DEC

Many thanks to my dear wife Phyl for the patience when reading through my manuscript and helping me with anything that is technical computer wise.

Also I don't think I would have written two books if Maurice Holloway hadn't invited me to join Paphos writers group. This group gave me so much encouragement and advice.

All Clenched Up and Finally Finished

Mick O'Reardon

Grosvenor House
Publishing Limited

This book is published by
Grosvenor House Publishing Ltd
Link House
140 The Broadway, Tolworth, Surrey, KT6 7HT.
www.grosvenorhousepublishing.co.uk

A CIP record for this book
is available from the British Library

ISBN 978-1-83615-070-1
eBook ISBN 978-1-83615-071-8

Acknowledgement

The front cover is a painting of me shoeing a horse in Northern Cyprus. The artist is Phyl O'Reardon, although I think she ran out of paint when painting my hair.

ALL CLENCHED UP AND "FINALLY" FINISHED

In my first book, *All Clenched up and Nearly Finished*, I told about my life and farrier life in Leicestershire from 1964 to 2004. After over 40 years of shoeing horses, Phyl, my wife, and I, had decided we could afford to retire to live in Cyprus. We had already bought a house there two years before, which we had used as a holiday home. When the time came for our flit to our new home, I expected to be searching for other projects to do but I was not expecting to shoe horses ever again. Phyl didn't really want to be an accountant anymore. She wanted to spend her retirement into her painting, which she hadn't done for years. I hadn't got a clue at the time what I would do with my days. One thing I can tell you is I wouldn't be sitting in an armchair, smoking a pipe with a flat cap on my head and wearing slippers. No, I don't smoke or own a flat cap, but I do own some slippers. I surprised myself. I started writing my books.

Reflections of my Farrier Life

In one way I felt sad that my 40-odd-year career as a farrier in Leicestershire have come to an end. Although I had a few obstacles that I had to overcome from starting work to ending a successful business, I must say I enjoyed the journey. I know one or two clients tried to do the dirty on me, but all the others were a pleasure to work for. Often, I still reflect on my days shoeing horses in the UK. Some clients I had known from when I first started work as an apprentice at Derek Spence's forge in 1964.

I enjoyed going to work and I got a great buzz when I got results with horses that had foot problems. I think of the first time I attended a horse on my own that was standing on three legs and bearing no weight on its off fore and pointing its toe towards the ground. I felt proud that I could help any animal and I had a sense of euphoria when I soon had a load of pus oozing out of an abscess. I got the same feeling, whatever the horse's problem right up till the day I retired. I lost count of horseshoes I had made that were not in any textbooks that helped a horse with foot or leg problems. Sometimes I had an idea of what was wrong before I got to see the horse, just by how the owner described the problem over the phone. Then there were the variety of surgical horseshoes I had made for different lameness. Bearing in mind farriers made all their own horseshoes in days gone by from scratch. Although there were one or two manufactured, ready-made horseshoes on the market, unfortunately they all needed work on them before they were acceptable to be fitted to the horse's hoof. In other words, it took nearly the same amount of time to make our own from scratch than to doctor these ready-mades. Also, it was a rewarding challenge to have constructed something which was not in any textbooks and to get results which helped a horse with foot or leg problems.

I can think of a time when making my own horseshoes worked to my advantage. One of my clients, who had enjoyed being transported around the countryside in her pony and trap wanted to broaden her driving experience to competing in driving competitions. She had got a new grey pony on loan, with a view to buy, ready for the challenge as her old pony was ready for retirement. This new pony was around 14.2 and it took 11-inch in length of steel to make the shoes. The pony was no trouble and behaved perfectly and the lady was happy with my work, although once or twice she thought she could pull the wool over my eyes. Fast forward to one week later, she rang me to inform me her pony had lost a shoe already and wanted the shoe replaced. I apologised if it was my work that led to the lost shoe and said I would call later in the morning.

When I arrived, I could see a grey pony in the stable with only three shoes on and no client in sight. Again, it was no trouble to tap the lost shoe back on and I left my charge nailed to the stable door. Later that day, I got an irate lady telling me I shouldn't be charging as it was less than week since I had attended to her pony. I told her, 'You are correct, it is less than a week when I shod your grey pony, but it wasn't the one I did today.'

'What do you mean? Do you think I have got two greys?' she replied in a stroppy voice.

'Well, if it is the same one as last week, its feet must have grown two sizes. Also, that is not my work as it looks like Joe South's work.' (Not his real name).

Making my horseshoes was like handwriting to me. With the best will in the world, no one person will make an exact copy of others in the same profession. Whatever skill one has, is not exactly like another with the same job. We have our own style. Also, this lady's second pony, which she had, again, got on loan, had been shod a lot longer than a week ago, more like six or seven weeks. It wasn't anything to do with Joe South's work either. The pony was ready to be shod. It didn't annoy me, it amused me – her thinking that she could pull the wool over my eyes to get out of paying. I am pleased to say she never tried it on again and she still had me to shoe for her right up to my retirement.

I would listen to clients if they felt things were not quite right with how their horses were moving or whatever, and I would see if there was anything I could do to help. Yes, over the years I am proud that I was able to help many a horse. Often it would involve a vet and between us we would discuss what we needed to do. I lost count of the times I sat at Chine House Vets looking at X-rays of horses' hooves and legs and chatting over a coffee about which surgical horseshoe or whatever we needed to do next.

There was one case of a lame horse which was owned by a very valued client of mine called Di. She rang me one bitterly cold, freezing Saturday morning when I was attending a farriers' meeting at Stoneleigh showground where the Farriers' Association head office is. At the time I was the chairman of the Leicestershire branch of farriers where I had to attend functions or discussions from time to time. That morning, Di rang me in a panic as one of her horses was hopping lame on its near side front leg. Again, from how she described the lameness, it sounded like a very ripe abscess which needed attention sooner rather than later.

I knew I wouldn't be able to help, but phoned my old farrier mate, Andy Speck, to see if he would be able to help. Sure enough, as soon as I told Andy of Di's horse's lameness, he thought the same as me: an abscess. With another stroke of luck, he had an appointment at one of his own clients in the village where Di lived that morning.

In the early evening, Andy rang me to update me to the reason why Di's horse was so lame, and it was totally different to what I was expecting. He said, 'Mick, I was sure I was going to find a very ripe abscess the way the horse was holding its front foot. There was not a hint of any abscess, but it did flinch when I squeezed the sole on the inside of the hoof. I couldn't find anything but in the gateway of the paddock, the ground looked all churned up, but the rough rugged ground is frozen solid now. I think it may have bruised its foot on the frozen ground. I told her to bathe the foot in salted warm water to bring out any bruising.'

'You could be right, Andy. Before the ground froze, the gateways were all churned up. Let's hope that is all it is and thank you for your help.'

First thing on Monday morning, I had Di on the phone again and her horse was not any better but looked to be getting more distressed. I thought it must be an abscess and Andy had examined it a day too early before the brewing abscess had developed. It can happen. I have witnessed it before where the horse owner has had the vet out but they can't find anything, then a couple of days later I have found a very ripe abscess, or I can't find the problem, but the vet does a day later.

I called at Di's later that morning and was sure I was going to find a foot full of pus and Di would tell me I was brilliant and think I was God. Well, it didn't happen like I thought it would. I was like Andy: I couldn't find any sign of an abscess either although it did flinch a little when I squeezed its sole on the inside of its foot. I advised Di to call her vet as I was of the opinion it could be more than a bruised foot. With the ground frozen solid, had the horse gone berserk when it was turned out into the paddock? Had it broken its pedal bone? All sorts of things were going through my head of what the problem could be.

That same day, in late afternoon, I got a phone call from Tom, a vet at Chine House. He said he had got Di's horse into their surgery, and I was expecting him to say the diagnoses was not good, but he didn't. He asked if I could call into the surgery as he had taken an X-ray of the horse's foot.

When I arrived, he said, 'Mick, I want you to have a good look at the X-ray of Di's horse's foot. While you are looking, I will get the kettle on.'

I had, over the years, studied many X-rays and could often see whatever the problem was and had made a variety of horseshoes to help different lameness. This one, though – I couldn't see anything that that would make a horse as lame as it was, and I said to Tom, 'I don't want to look a prat, but I can't see anything wrong,' thinking I had missed something quite obvious.

'I can't see anything wrong either. I was hoping you would have an idea,' replied Tom.

Over the coffee, we discussed this and that, thinking of what may be wrong. Both of us must have looked at the X-ray God knows how many times together. I then said to Tom, 'Let's get the horse into your examination room and go for gold. Let's hope it's a pocket of pus somewhere that's not showing up on the X-ray. I will sharpen my best searcher (knife) up.'

Although it was pitch dark outside, this examination room was lit up better than daylight. I had told Tom the horse flinched on the sole on the inside of its hoof but there was no sign of any puncture wound or the usual black mark that may give a clue an abscess was ready to pop. He had conducted the same examination as Andy and myself. I suppose it was just natural for us to concentrate on the horse's foot where it didn't like us exploring. I thought to examine the outside too, although again there was not any signs of a puncture wound or the usual marks that can give a clue to an abscess. I scraped my knife over the sole and as I did, I thought I heard a squelching sound. The point I heard this sound, I went for gold and dug deeper, and, to our relief, the eruption of a pus pocket I had hit was unbelievable. In all the years I had shod horses, I had never imagined a horse's hoof could hold so much pus.

Tom was sweeping all this infection down the drain. What surprised us was that the horse didn't flinch when we squeezed its foot where the abscess was. It flinched where it wasn't.

We must have spent a good hour examining the problem. Tom investigated further and found the infection went under the pedal bone, which must have caused a radiated pain. That would explain why the horse flinched on the inside of its hoof instead of the outside. Having had to dig out a good majority of its sole to get at the infection, I had to make a shoe up that evening where a plate could be screwed on and off to change the dressing daily. We were hoping the infection hadn't damaged the pedal bone but that was fine and thankfully the horse made a full recovery.

The farrier's van

I often think about when I started my apprenticeship at Derek Spence's and how things have changed. For example, the farrier's work van. In 1964, Derek, my old boss, had an old type minivan (although new at the time) to carry our farrier kit. All we had was our box of tools, a stand, and a small anvil for altering the shoes cold. We didn't carry a big selection of readymade horseshoes then as there were hardly any on the market, unlike today. We had to make the shoes for each horse we shod. If a customer booked us to shoe their horse, we had a notebook with the client's name and what their horse or horses were called, with the size of the horseshoe that was needed. Also, most horses were shod cold unless they were brought to the forge. Saying that, I have read an article about a guy who had his anvil, tools and small coke forge in a motorbike and side car in the 1950s.

Nowadays, an old type minivan would struggle to get a quarter of the kit a modern-day farrier carries. Even when I started my own in business in 1976 with my good mate Andy Speck, our mode of transport was an old Ford Anglia van. By then, mobile gas forges had just come on the market, and they took a bit more room up, but it didn't fill the motor to capacity. In those days, horseshoeing away from the forge was kept simple.

It had to as we didn't have the room for electric welders and grinders and God knows what other tools to make our work easier. Not to mention the stock of ready-made horseshoes, pads, tubes of vet-tech and many other aids that help a horse's comfort.

I often think of my old farrier mate, Brian Porter. His motor was a Lada estate car when he retired in 1998. He only carried his toolbox, a small anvil and the shoes he had made for that day's work, the same as when I started work in 1964. He was of the old school and even though he shod the horse's cold, I bet none of the horsey folk, or, for that matter, other farriers either, would have known. He was a respected guy in the profession as he gave lots of young farriers just starting out valuable tuition. His farrier life never seemed to have the problems that lots of farriers I see have today. Sometimes I start to think one or two farriers today seem to complicate diagnoses when there are none to diagnose.

I once got told a story off a well-known horse man at the time, called Eric Wright, about Brian and his dad arriving to shoe his horses on the bus in the 1950s. They had boarded the bus with their box of tools and stand, which was to rest the horse's leg on when clenching up. Eric told me he had got six or seven horses to shoe at the time. When they arrived at Eric's stables, Brian started with the horses at one end of the yard, removing the old shoes and dressing the hooves ready for his dad to fit. At the other end of the yard, Brian's dad had started to remove the horses' shoes ready for

Brian to fit. When they met in the middle, Brian's dad said, 'I thought you were doing the fitting, Brian.'

'You have the shoes. I thought you were,' replied Brian.

'I haven't got the shoes. Didn't you pick up what we had made off the forge's floor?' mutters Brian's dad.

'No, I didn't pick them up. You didn't tell me to,' says Brian.

Eric told me this conversation must have gone on between them for a good ten minutes. Neither of them wanted to take the blame for leaving the horseshoes at their forge. So they both caught the next bus back to their forge with their kit too. Eric didn't think they had thought it would have been best to leave their tools with him, and instead lugged them back and forth on the bus. I think keeping it that simple nowadays is perhaps going a bit too far.

Another farrier who I will call Jed (not his real name) got his clients to pick him up when they wanted their horses shod because he had never learnt to drive. When he had finished at one stable, the next client for his next port of call would arrive to transport him to their stables. So, again, he would have just had the basic equipment that would have had to fit into a car boot. Jed never seemed to have any problems either and was very popular amongst his clients. The odd time Jed didn't need his clients to pick him up was when he asked for help from his farrier friends when he had a busy day. He would often ask other farriers, including me, to give him a hand on days when he had too much work on.

When I helped him, I got the feeling he was well thought of, especially amongst his lady clients. None seemed to mind picking him up. Jed was like my old mate Brian Porter, who could get away with rude, playful, sexy banter to lady clients, who would laugh and joke with him. I often thought if I said the same words, I would have got slapped in the face for being rude.

I can remember a time when I had first started out in business and was thankful for any work, when Jed asked me if I could help him out as he got a lot on. At one call, one of his lady clients, who I will call Maggie, had told Jed she wouldn't be able to pick him up as her car was in the garage for a repair. He told her I was helping him, and I had a van and did she want us to pick her up from her home as her horse was stabled two or three miles away. It was the time I had the old Ford Anglia van so you can imagine with both my and Jed's tools plus an anvil and a mobile forge, it was quite full. When he told me we had to pick Maggie up, I thought he would just squash himself in the back of the van amongst the tools. When we arrived at Maggie's house, she was already waiting outside. As soon as I had stopped Maggie opened the passenger door and before Jed had chance to move, she said she would sit on his knee. Again, Jed said something that was of the sexy nature and got a reply along the same lines back. If it gave an old man a thrill, did it matter? On the journey to the stables, and after negotiating a cattle grid, Jed shouted, 'Mick, stop, stop and back up,' in a loud voice.

I thought I had missed a turning to the stables as they were directing me. 'I haven't seen a turn off, Jed. Have I gone too far?' I replied.

'No but can you back up over the cattle grid quickly, then shoot forward over it fast,' shouted Jed.

'What for?' I asked.

'Ooh, just for the thrill of it, especially with Maggie sitting on my knee,' an excited Jed stuttered, which made Maggie laugh and give Jed a dig in the ribs with her elbow, and some playful banter back.

Farrier's equipment

I mentioned my mode of transport when I started out in business was an old Ford Anglia van. At the time, it seemed big enough for my tools and horseshoes, even larger than Derek's minivan. Nowadays the vans and farrier rigs have got much larger to cope with the equipment. I often think that old Anglia van would never have coped with the stuff I see in vans today. I have spoken with other farriers around the same age as me about what they think of some of the younger farrier generation (I am 76 years old at the time of writing). I found a lot agreed with me that they had shod the same horses for years without having to fit 3d pads and bar shoes and so forth. I am not saying these products are a bad thing because they are good when the horse does have a serious problem. I am not against horses having pads and special remedial shoes as I have fitted them myself after a discussion with a vet and owner. What I had witnessed was that some farriers just fitted them willy-nilly and assumed the horse would have a lameness problem, without discussing the problem either with the client or with a vet.

I can remember a horse that had these pads fitted with wonderful ironwork nailed to its foot. Again, this horse owner, who I will call Jessy, didn't know her horse had a problem until she moved to new stables in an area her old farrier didn't cover. Her old farrier had shod her horses for years and in her eyes did work to her satisfaction. The new farrier, who did most of the new stable's shoeing, said her horse needed pads and egg bar shoes with a rubbery substance (Jessy's words, not mine) to be squirted under the pad. He hadn't trotted the horse out to see how it moved or to see if it suffered from a slight lameness. Jessy didn't seem to have much say on how her horse was going to be shod. As she put it to me when she asked for my opinion, she felt he was saying, 'Sod what the owner wants. He was going to do my own thing regardless.'

Over the years I had heard similar sorts of remarks before from other horse owners. I agreed with Jessy that I had a feeling her horse's shoeing technique didn't need to be changed. If it wasn't broken why change it? Her horse was moving soundly before and had never had any foot problems in all the years she had owned her faithful friend. Now it had got God knows what fitted and she felt its conformation wasn't how it used to be.

When I was asked for my opinion, I told her I would fit a normal set of shoes like her original farrier did, and we would go from there. Mind you, I was praying I had done the right thing as sometimes some horsey folk don't tell the true story of what has happened to their horse in the past. This time though I had the gut feeling Jessy was being honest with me. Although I enjoyed doing remedial work, I would have discussed the problem with both vet and client. By then, I had probably studied X-rays with the vet and we both would have discussed the best way to tackle a problem first. Sure enough, all that Jessy's horse needed was a normal set of shoes and the horse was still going strong when I retired to live in Cyprus a couple of years later.

Three or four years later, when we came back to the UK for a holiday, I bumped into Jessy and she told me she had changed her farrier several times since I had left and wished she could have me or her first farrier to shoe her horse.

....

I knew another guy, who I will call Den (not his real name), who years ago did his farrier round with his horse and cart. Mind you, this was 60 to 70 years ago. He was a jolly sort of chap and well liked amongst the horsey folk. The trouble was he often called at his local when he finished his day's work. I had heard many a tale of how Den liked a Guinness or two or three or four! Den's old horse would wait patiently for him, tied up in the pub's carpark. Unfortunately, Den often needed a little help to get him to his horse and cart when he left. All the locals who knew Den would help him into his cart and the old horse would head for home without Den's help. The old nag had got used to this routine and just knew – he didn't need his master's help to negotiate the road back home.

Nowadays, I see farrier vans laden down with kit that the old school wouldn't have thought about and would never have used. Over the years I have seen a variety of a brands of machine-made horseshoes come and go on the market and disappear like the latest trendy clothes fashions do. They get used for a while and disappear, never to be seen again. I used to joke with my old mate, Brian Porter, about the latest horseshoe fashion that was on the market. A bit like the human race with the latest clothing that arrived in the shops. When we made all our own horseshoes, I noticed we did more work with the hammer to box out the heels or whatever so very little rasping and filing was needed.

In Cyprus I met a Cypriot farrier whose van was full to the brim with tools he would never use in his lifetime. I say he wouldn't use them because he had no idea how to make a basic horseshoe, let alone a surgical one. He had only fitted machine-made horseshoes and told me horses didn't need remedial shoeing, so why did he need to cart all this gear around?

NAVICULAR DISEASE?

Another client of mine, who I will call Diane, had more or less been given a horse I will call Daisy. The previous owner was told that Daisy had the start of navicular disease, and she tripped now and then. On my first shoeing appointment, I asked Diane, 'Who diagnosed navicular disease? A vet?'

'The last owner's horsey mate was certain it had it,' Diane muttered.

So how would I go about shoeing Daisy? All I did was not dress the heels too low and kept the toe short and instead of a clip at the toe of the shoe, I rolled it to help the break over to help with the tripping. After shoeing Daisy for four or five years, and this "navicular disease" not getting any worse, Diane moved stables to miles out of my area.

Diane's and Daisy's problems started when she got another farrier to shoe her horse at the stables she had moved to. The poor woman was told her horse would be dead in six months if it was shod the way I had done it. After dressing the feet and lowering the heels, he got out of his van a selection of surgical shoes and spent a few minutes deciding which ones would be best. Then more time was needed on which pads would be best to be fitted under the shoe. He then got out (a Jessy quote) a tube of a rubbery substance to be squirted under the pad to stop concussion.

Six weeks after Diane had her horse shod by her new farrier, I got a phone call from her one evening. She was pleading with me that if I wouldn't travel to her new yard, could she bring her horse over to my forge. Instead of making her horse more comfortable foot-wise and to extend its life beyond six months, it never felt comfortable when she rode. Not only that, what she was charged, with all the extras, she felt she had been ripped off.

I told Diane if she could get her horse over to me, I would see what I could do. A few days later she arrived at my forge with her horse and I had a good idea why the conformation could be better. With the heels dressed far too low and the toe too long, I told her I would shoe how I always did and to go from there. A few days later, Diane got in touch to say her old horse was moving much better without any remedial shoeing and if she couldn't find another farrier who would shoe like me, she was prepared to box her horse over to me.

A couple of weeks after I shod Diane's horse, I was duty farrier at the Leicester county show. Also, the Leicestershire farrier branch also held a farrier competition which I helped to organise. I had noticed this young guy kept looking in my direction and eventually came up to me. He had some remarkable photos of how he had shod Diane's horse and was keen to try to show me up in front of his mates about how good he was. I looked at the photos and said, 'That's some mighty impressive work you have done there. There is one problem though.'

'What's the problem?' he asked.

'Well, it would have been a lot better if you had shod the horse instead of sticking four shoes on,' I replied, as he didn't know I had shod Diane's horse since.

'I had to shoe it that way or it could have big problems later,' he replied with a big smirk on his face, sure he was doing his best to belittle me in front of his mates.

I know I probably should have told him sooner what I knew but I suppose I let him be on his high horse before I told him he wasn't going to be shoeing Diane's horse ever again. When I finally told him that she had brought her horse over to me as she told me, in her words, he had conned her and spoke a lot of bullshit. I could see his face change colour when he found Diane was not happy with his work. I did tell him if he was going to enjoy bragging in front of his pals, he wanted to make sure his client was happy with his work first. I don't like folk who try to show others up in front of their friends as I can assure them one day the boot may be on the other foot. I didn't mind getting ideas off other farriers when there were problems as that is what farriers did years ago. Farriers I knew years ago would never tell a client that they were better than others. We prided ourselves on our work and that was our advertisement. If a client didn't like your work, you made sure you pulled socks up so it didn't happen again.

That was one example about trying and keep the job as simple as possible and I have always said, in my opinion, when I didn't know the full facts about a new horse or client because there may be a reason why the remedial work was required. The other was don't try to show me up, especially when your idea didn't work. I am not saying there is no needs for pads and glue, and God knows what else, but my motto is if it isn't broken, don't try to fix it. More than likely it will break then.

My point is, do we need a massive motor to cart all our equipment about? It may just be my opinion and others may agree or disagree. I accept what works for one guy doesn't work for another. I have read reports of the police targeting vans in general for being overweight. If it is over they will not let you leave until the extra weight is unloaded. Brian Porter kept everything simple and he shod his same clients' horses for years without any fuss. Granted, I did shoe hot from a mobile gas forge, but I never once carried a grinder to box the heels off and other equipment. I moulded the shoe while the iron was hot with my hammer with very little rasping needed. I have seen farriers rasping at the heels of a shoe until sweat was dripping off the end of their nose. I don't know if that gives them a clue to stop the filing. I found it a lot easier to shape up with the hammer while the metal is hot. I know I did use a transit van in later years and I did have more equipment than Brian's Lada estate car, but I did invest in more machine-made shoes when the end product got better. So I suppose I did carry a little more stock but nothing like what I see in farrier vans today. I still tried to keep the job as simple as possible and never had the problems I hear about today.

Amusing, and not so amusing, moments

I still think about amusing moments and not so amusing episodes that have happened in my life as a farrier. I can remember shoeing for a lady I will call Mrs Giles who I had shod for many years. She was a lovely lady with a very refined voice. The lads who worked for me at the time would be careful to watch their Ps and Qs when they spoke. Well, we soon realised we needn't have bothered. Mrs Giles could swear like a trooper and she knew better dirty jokes than we did. I suppose at first she was like us – she was watching her language until she got to know us too. Her old horse, called Bengy, was brilliant to shoe and we knew he was getting on in years. We never questioned her, but at most visits over the years, she would tell me Bengy was 15 years old. He was an amazing horse, because he stayed the same age for many years.

After being 15 for a few more years, Bengy started to get a little fidgety. A year later it was a case of someone holding onto him when he was shod, as he refused to be tied up. Mrs Giles was having the same problem when she wanted to groom him or whatever. He would run back and struggle until either he would break the head collar or continue to struggle until he was free. Another six months later it got downright dangerous not only to shoe but to groom and he had become difficult to ride as Mrs Giles found out one morning while out on her hack.

Without warning, Bengy took off like a Grand National winner and threw Mrs Giles to the ground. Luckily, she was not seriously hurt apart from her pride and one or two bruises. For Bengy, it was another story. A farmer saw him galloping flat out down the road and he didn't look like stopping for anyone. A mile or so later at a T-junction, he didn't turn the corner but ran straight ahead into someone's garden and demolished a wooden fence on the way in. He only stopped when he hit the wall of a house and died at the scene. It is thought he had had a brainstorm which is more likely, judging by his erratic behaviour. I felt sorry for him as for most of his life he was a pleasure to have as a client. I think if the truth was known, he was nearer to 25 years old and, the same as in humans, old age caught up with him.

Then there was Mrs Horrocks who could make me late if I wasn't careful, or even if I was. Her hospitality was a little too welcoming. At most calls, clients made a hot beverage while I shod their horses. I would drink my mug of tea but carry on working. Mrs Horrocks, though, would wait until I shod her horse and would want to chat to me while having a coffee with her in her kitchen. Every time I went to shoe her horse, I would say to myself several times, *I must not stop for a coffee at Mrs Horrocks'*. Even when I had started shoeing her horse, my head would be saying, *for Christ's sake, don't get talked into having a coffee.* The same again when I got the horse shod, my brain would be saying, *I have not got time as I will be late for my next appointment.* Yes, you can guess, Mrs Horrocks managed to convince me I had time for a coffee even though I was convinced I hadn't.

The times I had sat in her kitchen thinking I shouldn't be there while she insisted on making a percolated coffee. Not a boiled kettle quick one. Yes, I still smile how she won every time. Mind you, she was always telling me I was the best farrier she ever had. I suppose it was something I liked to hear, not giving it a thought that other farriers have had the same remarks off their clients too.

. . . .

Mrs Ann Harris and her husband, Peter, were very valued clients who I had shod for many years. Ann always had their two ponies ready for me at their little bungalow on a concrete base next to her garage. If the weather had caused her paddocks to be a bit muddy, she would apologise to me and say, 'Sorry about the mud and the state of the hooves, Mick.'

'No need to apologise, Ann. We are not in the paddock,' I would reply.

'I have tried my best to clean them before you arrived,' muttered Ann.

'If you can see any mud on your pony's hooves, you have better eyesight than me, Ann, I can't see any,' was my reply.

Well, some folk would question why she needed to apologise. Surely the horse owner should do that for their farrier, even though lots didn't? Well, Ann was nearly blind with a hereditary eye complaint that ran in her family. Her pony's hooves and legs were always spotless. Even if there were bits she had missed, I wouldn't have moaned about it like I did at other calls where there was no eyesight trouble. Also, the photo on the front cover on my first book, *All Clenched Up and Nearly Finished* is a photo of me shoeing Ruby, one of Ann and Peter's ponies. What is even more remarkable about that is Ann took the photo with very limited vision in one eye. Yes, she was a lady I really admired. I was always greeted with a smile and mugs of tea and an apple pie she had made. I once said to her that she was a brave lady not just to ride her pony, but because she also competed in gymkhanas.

I can still hear her say, 'The pony can see where it is going, I can't.'

Sadly, Ann did lose her sight and an old farrier friend, Luke Brown, who took on shoeing Ann and Peter's ponies after I retired to Cyprus, told me years later, 'Do you know, Mick, Ann still rides.'

I suppose it didn't surprise me as she was one hell of a lady with a heart of gold and a determination to succeed no matter what obstacle she faced. Luke had looked after Peter and Ann's ponies from the day I retired to Cyprus until the present day (20 years) and found Ann and Peter to be wonderful clients like I did.

THE WINTER ELEMENTS

What I wouldn't miss, though, after retiring to Cyprus, was working in the rain, wind, or whatever winter elements decided to erupt while halfway through shoeing a horse. The times I had got drenched when nowhere near finished with no shelter when the heavens open. It was not just a matter of getting soaked – the rasp tended to clog up when it got wet. Your hands and tools got slimy and the job seemed to go on forever.

I can remember a time years ago when Willy Williams worked for me. The day that sticks in my mind was where we had got several calls and it was a dull and cloudy day. We sensed some foul weather was brewing the way the breeze was changing into a cold wind and we hoped we wouldn't get caught out by it. That day on our round we had two horses booked in which were not on a stable yard. The only call with no stables or shelter. The gateway of the paddock the horses lived in was up to the neck in mud but luckily the gate opening was onto the end of a no through road. The lady who owned the horses had them both tied up to the gate and was waiting on the roadside when we arrived. She had cleaned her horses' muddy feet and legs ready for us. With no traffic, we didn't see a problem and at least we had a hard clean surface to work on. We didn't waste any time and got stuck in, when one of us said, 'Hope the rain holds off until we have finished, it looks mighty black.'

Well, the rain did hold off! It snowed instead! First a few flurries, which didn't bother us too much. Before we were halfway through, the few snow flurries had got faster and had turned into a raging blizzard. Plus the wind chill seemed to go down to be minus-blooming-Moscow. The poor woman was so cold she started to shiver. We told her to get in the back of my van and warm herself up next to the gas forge. How we got those two horses shod I will never know. Willy and I looked like snowmen but both horses were as good as gold and seemed quite happy munching on their hay nets, unaffected by how hard it was snowing and how cold it got.

DIFFICULT HORSES

'He didn't mean to kick you and he was OK with the last farrier,' I have this heard countless times, or words to that effect. Bigger alarms bells sounded when some owners would say, 'I am sure you will get on better without me helping you.' That could mean the nag is a right bastard to shoe and they were scared to help you and they didn't want to get hurt. I think I can say most farriers have had something similar said to them. Folk should realise that us farriers talk to each other, not just in the county where we reside but throughout the country. Sometimes from abroad too, the world is small now with just a click of a button.

I would say 95% of my clients wouldn't have put me in any danger but there were the odd ones who couldn't care less if the farrier got injured. Some horsey clients think it is the farrier's job to train their horses, to pick their nags' feet and more or less school their unruly horses. Some owners never give it a thought that the farrier job is hard enough physically without having to tangle with an unschooled horse. I used to allow an hour to shoe the horse but when the client expected me to school their horse too, it would no doubt make me late for my next appointment. Yes, I agree there are horses on the nervous side or a youngster which needs a little gentle fuss while they are shod for the first time, but I am not talking about them. It's the plain nasty ones that no one has ever managed to tame and sometimes the behaviour was no better when they were 10-plus years old. The times I have asked for advice off previous farriers about some unruly horse and got told a totally different story from what the client told me.

It is no good blaming the farrier that the horse is difficult to shoe. It is the owner's responsibility to train their horses. They need handling daily from the day they are born. Not once every six weeks or so when it is time for the farrier. I have heard several folk over the years say they had waited until I came to pick up a youngster's feet, especially the hind legs. Well, the owner ought to have been doing that every day so the animal got used to it. Doing it once every six weeks, or in some cases months, the horse gets it into its head trimming and shoeing is mess-about time. I can think of owners over the years who never touched the hind legs as the horse kicked. Some were just left to run wild in a 40-acre field from the day they were born. Then, four years later, the owner decides the horse needs to be broken in to ride. By then, their youngster has got stronger and it's probably got into its head it is not too keen for any sort of discipline. Horses and ponies can use their strength against a human no matter how strong the human is.

....

Even quiet horses can have their moment. To give an example of how a horse can be stronger than a human, I can remember one case of a couple I will call Jane and Robin. Jane owned a flimsy little Arab called Bella

(Robin's description, not mine). I must say Bella was very well behaved for me to shoe and was a pleasure to have as a client. Robin, though, was a sod for wrapping the lead rope around his hands when he led the horse out of the stable or field. I had often told him he shouldn't do that in case the animal got spooked or whatever and took off as he wouldn't be able to let go.

I have, over the years, seen very docile animals, like Bella, having their moments. It only takes a discarded plastic bag rustling in the wind to spook a horse. I can remember years ago a farrier getting badly hurt shoeing a horse that hadn't got a vice in its head. That happened when the horse was taken into a barn to be shod due to a thunderstorm. The horse was standing perfect and probably half asleep. Then a bird that had been roosting up in the rafters decided to move. It flew around the barn flapping near the horse's head and spooked the animal, causing it to knock the poor farrier to the ground. The way I would describe it is, imagine if you are sitting in your armchair and half asleep. Then somebody gives you a shake on your arm – it would probably make you jump by being taken by surprise. It may make you flap your arms. Well, it's the same thing with animals. Before the horse realised what was happening, first a bird flapping around its head. Then, after knocking the farrier to the ground from getting startled, caused more confusion under its hooves. That farrier ended up with a broken leg and other injuries caused by a bird flying near the horse's head. So even with bomb-proof horses the unexpected can happen.

Getting back to Robin, the unexpected did happen to him. I know when you're leading a horse and something spooks it, you will try to hang on to it but with the best will in the world, things don't always work out like that. With the rope wrapped around Robin's hands and a horse deciding to gallop off, he could get seriously hurt from not being able to let go.

Robin seemed to think he would be able to control Bella, no matter what. His reply to me was, 'A flimsy little Arab is not going to get the better of me.'

Well, Robin was a big strong chap. He stood six-foot-six in height with a muscular body to match. I for one wouldn't have wanted to argue with him. Well, this flimsy little Arab did argue with him about who was the strongest, and it wasn't Robin who won. He had accompanied Jane to a show where she was competing. Robin, who didn't ride but enjoyed supporting his wife, was leading Bella past a practice arena with one or two jumps erected. A plastic bag flapped in the wind and spooked Bella. This flimsy Arab took off at great speed and of course so did Robin. He got no choice as the lead rope was wrapped around his hand. Bella headed into the practice area, and with a stroke of luck, another jockey came to Robin's aid to stop Bella charging off. He told me he had visions of him bouncing along the ground as Bella was galloping off a lot faster than he could run with his feet trailing in the air.

Robin admitted it was his own fault and said, 'Mick, the times I never listened to you. I thought I was a big strong chap but my strength didn't come close to matching a flimsy little Arab. I felt like a flimsy little bloke getting tossed around like a rag doll. When Bella shot off into the practice arena, I was terrified she would go over one of the jumps and I wouldn't be able to let go if I wanted to. I would have had no option to jump the jumps too. It taught me horses, and little flimsy things too, are stronger than me.'

I couldn't resist asking Robin, 'If Bella had jumped a few jumps and you had had to too, do you think you would have managed a clear round?'

WILD HORSES

I have witnessed horses being schooled by folk who are novices. They think they know what there are doing but all that is happening is the horse or pony is getting more out of hand. I am sure I can speak for most farriers that we all would sooner shoe two good horses than one bad one that takes twice as long. I got lucky at the end of my career. I could afford to pick and choose and had wheedled out any bad payers and plain dangerous horses.

I had the case of a women years ago, who I will call Mrs Dewhurst (not her real name). She would buy or take on a horse that no one had ever managed to school or ride, because they were more or less being given away. Her idea was buy cheap and with a bit of schooling she thought she could make lots of money. I am not talking about a young horse that has not yet been broken or even one that was on the nervous side. I am talking about horses who, no matter how good a schooling they have had, are still plain dangerous to ride or to be around. I know some horses in the right hands have become of a better nature but when something that is 10-plus years old and had no sign of improvement, alarm bells rang in my ears.

Mrs Dewhurst, who took these horses on, was an accident waiting to happen, but it wouldn't be her who had the accident. She employed a young girl that was on, at the time, a scheme called YTS (Youth Training Scheme.) This young lass, who I will call Brenda (again, not her real name), was brilliant at handling these wild horses. Much better than her boss. I doubt she ever learnt much from her boss who employed her anyway. Mrs Dewhurst didn't get herself within an arm's length of anything that looked dangerous.

I can remember a time when Brenda phoned me one evening to warn me that it was her day off when Mrs Dewhurst had me booked to shoe a new horse. She warned me this new horse was mad and not to try to shoe it without someone holding onto it. Brenda had the idea that her boss would say what she usually did when the going got tough, which was, 'I think you will get on better without me being around,' meaning, *I am terrified to help and I am not going to be the one who gets hurt.* From what Brenda told me that evening, I had made up my mind to walk away if nobody was going to be able to hold the horse, although I didn't fancy Mrs Dewhurst. She was a woman who would try telling me what to do even if it meant it was my head that was going to get booted. I was still willing to have ago if she had organised somebody else more experienced to help me instead of herself.

Sure enough, when I arrived, I heard the favourite words off Mrs Dewhurst: 'I think you will get on much better without me!' When I told her I wasn't going to attempt to shoe the horse unless I got help, Mrs Dewhurst decided that she would help but wanted to hold the horse's lead rope over the stable door and to be outside the stable with me and the horse on the inside. I told her she had to come into the stable with me and the horse, or I walk away. That is what I ended up doing and put my tools back in my van and left because she didn't like my idea. I thought to let her get another farrier do her mad horses.

The extra time it took to shoe a wild horse and charge a bigger fee still left a farrier out of pocket. Then I have had folk moan at me that I am robbing them for charging more. I made more money shoeing well behaved horses for less money, than wild ones.

....

One Saturday night, at 11 o'clock, I got a phone call off a guy who was not one of my clients and lived miles out of my area. He asked me if I was up for a challenge. When I asked what the challenge was and it had better be a good one at that time of night, he replied, 'Are you interested in shoeing a very difficult horse?'

Well, that was the wrong thing to say to me at 11 o'clock on a Saturday night and my answer was, 'No, I don't like those challenges.' Then he told me that it was an emergency and important that his horse be shod by Monday. 'Well, that's your problem not mine,' was my reply.

It made me wonder how many other farriers he had rung that were local for him. Did other farriers not like the challenge either? The other thing – why did it become an emergency at 11 o'clock on a Saturday night? Or was it that farriers local to him knew too much about the horse and owner? At the time I had cut my work down to a ten-mile radius of home. Why on earth would I want to travel miles to shoe a difficult horse for a challenge when I had got more than enough well-behaved horses to shoe on my doorstep?

SCANDAL

Sometimes on the rounds we got to hear of a scandal that happened here and there. Over the years, I got to hear about who was having an affair with who. Sometimes it would be only a rumour, other times it was probably true. One day, a lady well known in the horsey world told me that her husband had left her for their groom. Well, I thought, these things happen, even though it was nearly 50 years ago when this happened. What was unusual about that then was the groom was male and it was a bigger thing than it is today to run off with someone of the same sex. I didn't know what to say until she told me she wasn't surprised and she had a feeling he preferred men to women, even though he never admitted it.

The groom, though, often boasted of his conquests to me with the opposite sex and what he liked to do to this lady and that lady. Sex seemed to be the only thing he wanted to talk about while I shod the horses. I suppose it took me a bit by surprise that he ended up running off with a man though. The two of them were still together 30-odd years later until the one of them suddenly passed away.

REPAYING HER SINS

'You'll never guess what I found out today,' said Willy Williams when he worked for me.

'Is it good or bad news?' I asked when he finished the farrier round I had sent him on.

'A bit of scandal. I caught a couple in the act of passion,' Willy muttered with his face lit up like a Christmas tree.

It was a day Willy had two horses to shoe at one of the day's appointments for a lady client who I will call Jenny (not her real name.) Jenny would have been in her late 40s to early 50s and lived on her own and spoke with a refined voice. She had never married and was a respected lady in the horse world. Her house and stables were in a very rural part of the Leicestershire countryside. Her property looked as if it could be a nice setting for an oil painting subject. The cottage had ivy crawling up the cottage wall and was surrounded by a variety of trees and mature bushes and shrubs in a well-kept garden. Leading out of the garden through a stone arch was a small stable yard which led onto a track back to the road.

Jenny owned two horses which had been off work for three or four months and out at grass. She was bringing them back into work and wanted their shoes back on. She had kept one of the horse's set of shoes when the shoes were taken off before they were turned out to grass as they were like new and just needed a refit. The other one needed new ones.

When Willy arrived at the appointment, he saw both horses were waiting in the stable. He did what we always had done and would nip up her garden and knock on her door to let Jenny know that he had arrived. Walking past a small window at the side of her house, and out of the corner of his eye, he caught sight of two folk with very little clothing on, who seemed to be passionately embracing each other. Now Willy didn't like to knock on the door to disturb them, so he did a quick retreat back to the stables. He decided to get started on the horse that needed new shoes and hoped the couple would be finished whatever they were up to before he needed the other horse's shoes Jenny still had. He was nearly finished shoeing the one that needed a new set and, to his relief, Jenny appeared with her man friend and apologised to Willy. She said, 'Sorry, Willy, never realised you had arrived. I was a bit busy,'

'Yes, I thought you must have been. Don't worry, I just started on this one,' muttered Willy, trying is best not to give a hint he knew what they were up to.

The thing, though, that startled Willy was Jenny's man friend was the local vicar. We were not sure if it was his way for her to repay her sins.

They are lots of the tales I could reminisce on and even to this day I have kept in touch with many old Leicestershire clients and was surprised how many folk bought my first book. I must thank you all who did, not just in Leicestershire but for the thousands who did worldwide. Now, though, I am going to enjoy early retirement and find a new hobby.

LEAVING FOR CYPRUS

The day finally arrived for our next adventure and both Phyl and I knew we were taking a chance seeing as neither of us were of retirement age. At the time we would have to live off our small private pensions topped up with our savings until we got our full pension. We had weighed up all the plusses and minuses and found the cost of living in Cyprus was a lot cheaper than the UK in 2004, although things did change a little when Cyprus joined the EU. I must say, giving two well paid jobs up was not easy and it did cross our minds whether we had done the right thing but sometimes life is all about chance.

The sale on our lovely home and forge in Leicestershire was completed by the end of August 2004, three weeks before we were due to depart for our next adventure. We were lucky that we had done a deal with the lovely folk who bought our house, and we could stay living in it for the three weeks before we moved.

I was still busy getting all our paperwork in order, which included passports for our dogs, Ben and Ally, ready. We had sold off most of our furniture and only kept one or two pieces that were of sentimental value. We didn't need to ship much out as our Cypriot home was already furnished from when we bought it two years earlier. A removal firm came and took the one or two bits of furniture we wanted to keep and other belongings to be shipped out to Cyprus. Mind you, that one or two bits were probably a bit more than we thought as it still filled a Luton-type truck. Now the house looked empty apart from a few clothes. We had negotiated a deal with the buyer of our house that included a double bed, a television, and a Welsh dresser, so at least we had still got a bed if nothing else until we departed. That was the deal so that we could stay in the house until our departure date.

What we had got left to take to Cyprus we could fit into two suitcases. Well, that was until I brushed past coats and fleeces still hanging on the coat rack that should have gone with the removals. The next day, one of us put something in the microwave and while it was heating the food we thought, *microwave, you should be on the way to Cyprus,* as our Cypriot home had not got one. Yes, that somehow had got missed like lots of other stuff, and we found we needed more than two suitcases. We needed four-plus.

Luckily, we had Phyl's sisters, Pat and Jacky, and their mother who had arranged to visit us a month after we had moved. They managed to pack their mother's clothes into their cases and bring one of ours. Phyl's daughter, Hazel, husband, Darren, and our granddaughter, Katy, had arranged to visit us a couple of months later and would bring the other.

So the day arrived for our flight for Cyprus. The dogs were on the same flight. We had to first find the drop-off place for Ben and Ally at 6:30 in the morning of September 22nd 2004 at Manchester airport. We were both a bit apprehensive about leaving the dogs although the firm who organised their travel had got Ben and

Ally's crates ready and waiting for them. It felt horrible leaving them, knowing they would have to spend four hours-plus in an aircraft hold. We were advised the dogs often felt more comfortable if some of our clothing was in the crates with them. I think my face lit up on hearing this as I thought about how many coats and fleeces would fit in with the dogs. Sadly, just one fleece each so the others would have to be draped over our arms as if we had just taken them off.

When we finally got to our check-in, we found pandemonium at the airport due to a security alert. The queue for passport control stretched, zig-zagging right through the check-in hall. I was glad we had arrived well before the recommended two hours before departure time. By looking at the slow-moving queue, we had a good idea it may take a good hour before we passed passport control and hand baggage search before we made it to the departure lounge. Also, I felt a bit of a fool with a load of coats draped over my arm on a warm September day, and then travelling to a country with an even hotter climate. I say coats as the biggest overcoats were trying to hide smaller fleeces underneath. As I have said, they should have gone in the container, like other stuff we had to cram into our overweight suitcases.

So we checked in with several overcoats draped over our arms pretending we had just taken them off. Then we had hand luggage 'cabin cases' that weighed about the same as a 20kg big suitcase. I was glad that hand luggage was on wheels. If I had to carry them I would have had difficulty pretending they were not heavy, especially with god knows how many coats draped over my arm.

At the check-in desk with our two very large bulky suitcases, we were prepared for an excess baggage charge as I could just about lift them on to the weighbridge. We knew both were way over the 20kg allowance. When one showed 36kg and the other 30kg, I was prepared for the worst news about how much we were going to have to fork out for being overweight. I was already getting my money out ready for a colossal charge. I saw the checkout lady count on her fingers as if she was working out what I had to pay, but she surprised me and said, 'Look, go to the back of the check-in hall and take 4kg out of the heaviest case and put 2kg into the other one and the other two into your hand baggage. We are not allowed to book anything over 32kg for health and safety. When you have done it, just come to the front of the queue as I have got the luggage tags and boarding cards ready.'

I thanked her and told her I would do that, trying my hardest not to show I had a big problem. I think the expression on Phyl's face could have given the game away if the check-in lady had noticed. As we walked away, struggling with our luggage, Phyl looked at me in a panic and I sensed hysterics brewing in her face. I had to tell her to go away and try to calm down while I sorted out what could go where, although I wasn't too sure either. She was sure we had got a problem and, to be honest, I was sure we had too. The last thing I needed was a hysterical woman with a raised voice yelling at me and possibly the rest of the airport hearing how we had a big problem. I had to be on my own while I was looking for a conclusion. The case we had to cram an extra 2kg into was a struggle to close when we first packed it the day before. How the hell was two more kilograms going to go into it? As for the hand baggage, we were already over twice the limit without other things to be crammed in. So I had to get Phyl to go out of the way while I repacked. The last thing a needed was a hysterical woman shouting, 'Mick, there isn't room for it, what are we going to do!' which in turn would attract attention.

I didn't know what was going to fit where, but it is surprising when one is desperate what one can do. Somehow, I did manage to stuff 2kg into the lightest case. Granted, probably one shoe went in one case and the other into a coat pocket. Yes, I knew all along the coats would come in handy as I filled all four coat and fleece pockets with 2kg of clothing.

When I had finished, I left Phyl with the hand baggage and coats and just took the two cases back to the check-in lady. I didn't want her to suddenly notice we were moving half a house. She hadn't seemed to notice we had got coats and fleeces draped over our arms. I still thought I was going to get hammered with a colossal amount as both cases were way over the 20kg limit. When the cases went on the weighbridge, I couldn't believe my eyes when both were spot on 32kg. I had just guessed that I had taken 4kg out of the heaviest case. I found the lady on the check-in was very nice when she said, 'That's fine, off you go and enjoy your flight,' as she handed me our boarding cards. So I quickly put my wallet back in my pocket before she changed her mind. I did as she said and quickly joined the long queue for passport control.

We had planned to have breakfast at the airport. On seeing a slow-moving queue for passport control and hand baggage search, we knew we may not have time. Phyl had spotted an outlet that sold sandwiches while in the check-in hall and had bought some sandwiches just in case. I was glad we had arrived in good time. Although we were prepared for a long wait, we didn't expect it to take two hours before we reached the departure lounge and found our flight gate had opened. We knew we hadn't any time to waste and trying to run or even walk quickly with our overweight hand baggage and coats was not easy. In the queue, some folk were complaining that they could miss their flights but it seemed to fall on deaf ears with airport staff.

When we finally got past the departure gate and onto the aircraft, I couldn't believe we had not been challenged, especially with a security alert. With our heavy hand luggage and coats draped over our arms we must have stuck out like a sore thumb. I have at other times been asked to cram something like a sweater into my luggage instead of over my arm. This time, though, no one said nothing about us having so much luggage when we moved to Cyprus. Luckily, we were at the very back of the aircraft and I managed to cram the coats in a space behind our seats. As for lifting the hand baggage into the overhead locker, I psyched myself up to lift the first cabin case into the locker, trying to pretend it wasn't heavy. Then I did the same with the other. Finally sitting in the seat, fastening the seat belt, I couldn't believe we were on the aircraft.

Then I thought of the dogs. Were they all right? Did the crew know they would be in the hold and was the heating switched on in the aircraft hold for them? If it wasn't they could freeze to death.

I had got to check before the aircraft was due to depart. I asked an air hostess if the crew knew our dogs were on board and was the heating switched on in the hold. She assured me they would be OK and she would check that they were on for me. A few minutes later she told me she had checked and the crew knew about them. They were already on the aircraft and she assured me that they would be warm throughout the flight. She then told me that they often carry animals and that other holiday travellers may be surprised what does go into the aircraft hold. She told me the tale of the one time they had six Alsatians on board. The dogs had been quiet until the aircraft got to the runway preparing to take off. As the engines revved ready to be thrust down the runway, one of the dogs must have barked and that set the others off howling. She said she heard passengers who were going on holiday say, 'Did you hear that, sounds like a load of dogs barking,' as they started to look out of the window, thinking they had escaped onto the runway. They were a little surprised that an aircraft had dogs on board going to their holiday destination.

Four and a half hours later we touched down on the runway at Paphos airport. We knew we were going to be met by someone from an animal rescue centre who had organised a vet as he had to check the dogs and that their microchip matched up to their passports. We found the office where these people had told us to go to. The lady from animal rescue told Phyl to stay with her and I had to collect our luggage. She would meet me at the front of the airport once the dogs had passed the vet and she would take us all home in her van. We were pleased for her kind offer as we hadn't got a clue how we going to transport all our luggage and two dogs plus their traveling crates to our home. Jim, our new neighbour, had said on an early visit if we were stuck he could help.

When the dogs got unloaded off the aircraft but were still in their crates, both of them were very quiet until they heard Phyl's voice. Then what a racket and I think it was a relief for them that we hadn't abandoned them. I didn't have to wait long before a white van appeared from the back of the terminal building with Phyl sitting in the front passenger seat. When we got home, I asked her, 'Did you go through passport control?'

'No one mentioned it. The dog lady just said jump in once the dogs were on board.'

'So are you an illegal immigrant.'

'I suppose I am, but after all the stress of today, I will keep quiet about that. It may cause more problems if we tell them.'

Ben and Ally were fine and I think the only thing on their minds once they were released from their crates was they both needed a big pee. Once they got to their new home and did a quick tour with a sniff here and there, the two dogs settled in as if they had lived there all their lives.

DONKEY SANCTUARY

On one of the visits for a holiday break before we retired full-time to our Cypriot home, we had become friends with our neighbours, Jim and Margaret. They mentioned to me when they were out one evening they had met a couple called John and Gill Powell who did work at the donkey sanctuary. They were concerned that the sanctuary was losing their farrier, and didn't know what they were going to do. Jim, a Cockney guy who had a wicked sense of humour, said, 'There is a guy who has just bought a house two doors from us. He is a farrier and I think he intends to move out to Cyprus full-time.'

'What, a qualified English farrier?' asks Gill.

'Yes, but I think he wants to retire, I will ask if you want.'

So when Jim told me the sanctuary was losing their farrier, Phyl and I decided to give this donkey sanctuary a visit in a village called Vouni. It was an hour's drive from our home at Chlorakas.

Mary and Patrick Skinner had started the sanctuary, first looking after a couple of donkeys which had then snowballed to 150-plus. They were not there when we arrived, but we met a lady who looked after the little gift shop that sold many items like t-shirts and other stuff to help with funds for the donkeys' upkeep.

When I told her who I was and what I did for living, she was straight on the phone to Mary. A few minutes later, a woman in a Mini Moke came charging down the track at great speed. Before her vehicle had hardly stopped, Mary leapt off and ran up to me, gave me a big hug and said, 'I feel you are an angel fallen out of the sky, we need you.'

They did have a guy, Phil, who helped out, who had had a crash course off George Hourie who was their Cypriot farrier. He had taught him the basics of trimming a donkey's hooves but, as I say, it was just basics. George had learned the trade off a respected English guy who at one time was an army farrier stationed in Cyprus. George was giving up farriery to concentrate on wrapping up his father's business affairs before all his family moved to New Zealand. So when Mary found out I was an English farrier with qualifications she couldn't believe her luck.

In Cyprus I found that if somebody's uncle taught their nephew one night how to shoe a horse, there was nothing to stop them starting up in business the next day as a qualified farrier. If it happens in the UK, it is an offence and a big fine. A four-year-four-month apprenticeship and a stiff examination of practical, theory and oral at the end is needed to be passed before one can set up in business as a farrier in the UK. Later on, I met some guys who said they were fully qualified and one had done a two-month course abroad, but there was no examination at the end. After two months, British farriers haven't scratched the surface of learning the profession, or is it we are slow learners?

OUR CAR

On our last holiday before we moved to Cyprus full-time, we had bought a little car! Unfortunately, the dealer insisted he wanted to give it a full service before we could take delivery and we were leaving for the UK later that day. Luckily, Chris, my eldest son, was going to be out on holiday the following week and we had arranged for him to pick the car up. I must say it came as a relief that the dealer was an honest guy and kept his side of the bargain with us having paid in full for the motor. He not only had the motor ready for Chris, but he was also only too happy to deliver it to our home.

I had mentioned to Jim we were a little worried about paying for the car before we had got it and then leaving the country and wondered if we had done the right thing. Then he told me a story of what happened to him before he and Margaret moved full-time to Cyprus. They had spotted some nice coffee tables at a little market outlet. Jim asked the stall holder, 'Do you always keep a stock of these coffee tables in as I would like to buy two? The trouble is we are leaving for the UK in the morning, but we will be back in three months' time.'

'Why don't you buy them today?' asked the stall holder.

'I can't. I haven't got enough money with me, but if you have them in three months, I'll buy them then.'

'Well, in that case, why don't you take them today and come and pay me when you are back in Cyprus.'

So Jim took the two coffee tables home and three months later, when he returned to Cyprus, he went back to pay the guy. The stall holder looked at Jim as if he didn't know him from Adam and asked if he could be of any assistance. 'I have come to pay for the coffee tables,' replied Jim.

'Oh, which coffee tables did you have and how much was I charging?' the puzzled-looking stall holder asked.

Jim did pay him and told me he felt the guy had forgotten, and in a Cockney accent said, 'Do you know, Mick, I could have made money dealing in bent coffee tables.'

Not that he would have done it. We trusted leaving him with a key as we also rented our home to holidaymakers before we lived there full-time. He and Margaret always washed the bed linen and kept an eye on the place for us. Also, car batteries can go flat quite easily, even after two weeks of not being used out there. So when Chris's holiday ended, Jim disconnected the battery and made sure it was fully charged when we arrived back.

FIRST DAY OF RETIREMENT

Sunday 23rd of September 2004 was the first day of "retirement" when we decided to give our car a run out and visit an open day at the donkey sanctuary. We hadn't even unpacked and had been in the country less than 24 hours. We had decided to give our car its first run out. Although covered in dust, we were surprised how well how our new motor ran. The dogs had gone on their morning walk and looked a little tired from what had happened to them over the last couple of days of travel. Both of them gave us the look as if to say, *can we stop at home now?* Both were curled up and were quite happy to stay put.

So we left the dogs at home and went to the donkey sanctuary. I kept saying to myself, *I must be mad as this retirement sounds to be short-lived. Has work come calling again? But I can't help not to be involved. My DNA will not allow me to give up my farrier life that easily.*

Although I didn't have to do anything that day, most folk involved with the sanctuary seemed to know who I was. I had packed a couple of paring knifes, rasp and clippers into our luggage as I got a good idea I may be starting work again sooner rather than later once we arrived. The rest of my farrier kit was being shipped out and wouldn't be arriving for a few weeks.

At the open day, Mary was so pleased to see me and I felt she was trying to introduce me to the whole of Cyprus who were connected to the sanctuary. By the time we left for home, I felt I knew not just the many folk connected to the donkey sanctuary but all the 150 donkeys too. I had got asked about what I would do with this ailment one donkey had and what I would do to others. I got the idea I ought to have qualified as a vet as well as a farrier. I found out then lots of Cypriot vets didn't specialise in equine although four or five years later there was a big improvement. I can remember the vet the sanctuary used in emergencies at the time. It had to be an emergency for two reasons. One was the expense as the sanctuary was on a tight budget. The other was the vet they had at the time looked frightened to death and very nervous if he got to within an arms-length of a donkey.

I had hardly had time to get settled into our Cypriot home when five days later, at 7:30 on a Friday morning, I found myself trimming donkey's feet. I could have started sooner as Mary had asked me if I could go on the Tuesday. We still had to unpack the suitcases and I had a few things I wanted to do at home first. I wanted a little time to relax after a stressful few weeks.

When I had got settled in, I was asked if I would attend on Tuesdays and Fridays. Phil, who had had a crash course off George Hourie, had done a good job keeping most of the donkeys' hooves in good order. The trouble was not all these donkeys had had a good life before they had arrived at the sanctuary. Lots suffered from laminitis and others suffered from grit getting up the white line of the hoof and causing an abscess. From what I gathered, this seemed to be a problem that occurred time after time with the same donkeys. I must say, the sanctuary recorded every ailment, no matter how big or small, of all the donkeys. For the never-ending abscesses, I thought of Vettec a type of glue that sets rock hard which farriers use for a variety of reasons. It can be moulded round the hoof like a shoe. I got a list of all the donkeys that kept getting abscesses and we would try squirting the Vettec around the foot to create a shoe.

The week before I was going to have ago with Vettec, George Hourie had called in and introduced himself to me. He was a jolly sort of chap and always seemed to be smiling as if he hadn't got a care in the world. He had never heard of this Vettec and took an interest in if it would work and would come back and give me a hand a week later.

Sure enough, a week later he did turn up to give a hand. Vettec did wonders as it cut abscesses down, although I had to use a bit of trial and error. In the UK when I used this glue substance, I would rasp it nice a smooth but in Cyprus I think the dry hot climate and the rugged terrain caused it to fall off a little too easily. I found making it look nice and tidy was not an option, but it was best to squirt plenty on plus more around the bottom outer edges of the outer wall of the foot and leave it. Rasping to make it look good seemed to weaken it. The donkeys didn't mind if it didn't look nice as it cured them of having a throbbing foot.

I suppose I didn't realise it at the time that I had become a vet as well as a farrier. I remember the time I attended to a donkey that had an abscess and put an Animalintex poultice on. Two weeks later, my sister-in-law, Jacky, was visiting us. Having a horse of her own, she was interested in coming with me to the sanctuary.

While I was trimming a donkey's foot, I got asked, 'Mick, when do we take the poultice off the donkey with the abscess?'

'Is pus still coming out?' I asked, thinking the worst.

'We don't know until the poultice is taken off,' came the reply.

'What do you mean? Is there pus in the poultice?'

They didn't know a poultice needed to be changed daily. This one had been left on for two weeks and I can still see the look of horror on Jacky's face. I just assumed when I applied the poultice that it would get changed daily. The other surprise was how well it had stayed on for two weeks.

GEORGE HOURIE

George's family were in the process of moving to New Zealand and although his parents had already relocated there, he had stayed to finalise the sale of the family's business. In the meantime, Phyl and I had become friends with George and his wife, Clare, and baby daughter, Lily, and a year later their son, George, was born. He had asked me if I would trim one of his old client's horse's hooves while he attended to the horse's teeth. He would meet us at our home and Phyl and I would follow him to Julie and Kleantihis near Polis. They had organised a barbeque at their home when we had finished attending to the horses. I think it may have been when we were chatting at Julie and Kleantihis that one of us mentioned Phyl was an accountant. It was just in a bit of banter about what we had left behind in the UK and now she was now helping out in a restaurant.

That job came by accident as she did it as a favour for Charles and Barbara who were near neighbours we had become friends with. They had for weeks worked hard to open a restaurant and on their first night were worried about being short of staff and asked Phyl to help out for one night only. OK, that one night lasted for two years but that was another story.

Weeks later, on a Sunday, Phyl left for a shift at the restaurant at 11 in the morning until around eight in the evening. On returning home shattered, she was greeted by George with paperwork in his hand. He had got in touch early in the week as he had remembered when at Julie and Kleantihis that Phyl was an accountant. He wanted her to look at some account figures. 'A relation is saying one of our family's companies owes them thousands in a business loan and we are sure we don't,' he said with a laugh and a smiley face.

I thought if somebody was accusing me of owing thousands to them, I wouldn't be having a jolly smile on my face.

Phyl looked exhausted but said to George, 'Look, give me 15 minutes and let me have a cup of tea first and I will see if I can sort you out.'

While we were having tea, George said his lawyers couldn't see any mistakes in the paperwork and wondered if Phyl could help. After she had her little rest, she looked at the figures and 20 minutes later she had sorted it and saw the mistake George's relation's bookkeeper had made and said to George, 'You do owe money – 98 Cyprus pounds,' and showed him the mistake.

'Oh, Phyl, now you've shown me it, how the hell did we all miss that? It is so obviously now. It's only taken you 20 minutes and all the rest of us have examined the documents for hours. Ninety-eight quid is better than the thousands which they were demanding!' he said with a bigger laugh as he said it.

A few days later when I met up with George, he gave me an envelope to give to Phyl with 50 Cyprus pounds in to thank her (it was before the euro). Phyl couldn't believe she got paid 50 quid for 20 minutes work as lots of office staff in Cyprus with qualifications in 2004/2005 were on £3 an hour. Also, she had just worked a nine-hour shift at the restaurant for a lot less than 50 quid.

Six months later, George asked me if Phyl would help him out again as the family's three companies' books had to be brought up to date before a sale of the companies could be agreed. I found there was a lot of land, not a few acres but miles and that was part of the sale of one company. I told him he was better off ringing her as I was in no position to say yes or no.

When I got home Phyl said, 'George is coming over with his family's three companies' books.'

'Yes, he asked me and I told him to ring you.'

Sure enough, George turned up with bags of documents and told Phyl about how his father had had an issue with the tax department nine years earlier and he wasn't going to do any more accounts until they sorted his complaint. So Phyl, in theory, had 27 years of books to sort out. Luckily, one of the businesses was tiny but to me there seemed to be a colossal amount of work. Anyway, she got stuck into it. OK, George had to come over now and then with other things she needed to know, but she finally got them finished to all the involved parties' satisfaction.

George had said work out what he owes her and that became a problem for us. I have said wages for office staff could be as low as £3 an hour in Cyprus then. Phyl must have spent God knows how many hours working on these accounts and worried that 850 Cyprus pounds might be too much. George, though, took that worry away from her a few days later before she presented him his bill. He said, 'Phyl, I've spoken to my father and seeing as one company is small (and a pause as if he was bracing to say a lower rate than Phyl's), would you be happy with two grand?'

Phyl was stuck for words. It was far more than she expected and eventually she squeaked, 'Yep.'

I couldn't believe that when we retired our work would still come running after both of us. I suppose I felt sorry that the donkey sanctuary was losing their farrier and then Phyl helping friends out at their restaurant and now doing accounts. Whatever was coming next? We had only been in the country less than a year and found work was looking for both of us.

DONKEY SANCTUARY OUTREACH

When I was asked to be the donkey sanctuary farrier, I didn't know they did an outreach program. This involved going to villages, often very rural places, where donkeys are still used, more amongst the old folk, for the harvest of grapes and carrying out various other tasks. I remember the first outreach I attended with John and Gill (the couple who had spoken to Jim about the sanctuary losing their farrier). They also became good friends of ours and at the time Gill worked full-time looking after the donkeys. We had gone to a village called Kallepia up in the hills near Paphos. I can't remember how many donkeys we attended to but it felt as if all the surrounding villages' folk had rounded up anybody with a donkey. Most of these people hadn't got any money as such and were probably scraping a living off their land. That was where their money was tied up – in a small bit of land. When the donkey sanctuary did this outreach program, most of these folk saw it as a way of getting their animals vetted and hooves trimmed for nothing, although the sanctuary was open to donations of what the donkey owners could afford.

That first day everything went like clockwork until the very last donkey. It was owned by a woman who looked to be in her 60s and her daughter, aged around 40, and neither looked the sharpest knives in the drawer. Their poor donkey could barely walk due to its hooves looking like Ali Baba feet. It was suffering from laminitis, plus many other problems. I don't know how long it took but eventually I got its hooves to nearer a normal length. Unfortunately, I found big abscesses in all four hooves. The poor thing must have been in agony. I thought it may be a waste of time putting an Animalintex poultice on as I knew it wouldn't get changed regularly. So we just bandaged its hooves up and told them we would need to see the donkey again the following week.

One of the locals who spoke a little English told us the woman didn't think the donkey had got a problem and was just lazy. She was pointing her finger to the side of her head with a little twist as if to say that these two were a sandwich short of a picnic. I thought, *oh dear, what is going to happen in a week's time? Are these two characters going to turn up with their donkey?*

The following week, accompanied by John, we turned up at the arranged time to see this donkey. I suppose we were expecting the worst and true enough there was no sign of the women or donkey. We didn't give up and John spotted the lady who could speak a little English. She told us the women were still trying to work their donkey and took us to their home. Again, I was still expecting a bit of hassle but the local did all the talking. She told us they would let us attend to their animal and just as I said, 'Where is it?' I saw it being led out of the front door of their house. Mind you, if you saw the house, it looked derelict and the washing on the clothes line looked dirtier than my working attire before it was washed.

I thought the donkey looked to be slightly more comfortable than when we saw it a week before but certainly nowhere near ready for work. Also, by some miracle, the bandaging was still on which surprised me but the poor thing had a long way to go to be anywhere near fit enough to work.

John and I did what we could and said we would call again six weeks later. Again, it was brought out of the front door and we could see a bit more of an improvement. I managed to trim by now nearly another two months of growth off its hooves and I thought we were making a little headway. I knew the sanctuary had got another outreach planned for that village and thought we would see this donkey then.

This next outreach appointment, the women didn't turn up with the donkey at the usual meeting point. Having other calls, we hadn't got time to go searching for them. I just assumed that with their donkey having so much wrong with it and from being neglected, the poor thing had passed away. A year later and back at Kallepia, the two women who missed their last appointments appeared, dragging their donkey which was in a desperate state. Far worse than the first time I attended to it. My heart sank at how it was forced to hobble up the street to us with all four hooves well overgrown. The poor thing was whacked on its backside with a stick and yelled at to make it walk. I knew whatever I did, it was not going to be enough, as it had developed other problems.

Also, the sanctuary had changed vets. Yiannis Pieroua was the new vet and took a lot more interest and had a lot more knowledge than the previous vet who came with us on these outreach appointments. When he saw this poor animal, he went mad with the owners. I don't quite know what was said in Greek but I got the idea he was giving the owners a right mouthful. The poor thing had difficulty standing when I tried to trim its foot. Yiannis sedated it to see if that helped. While I was making slow progress trimming its hooves, Yiannis and the two women were still in deep argument. While I was trying to trim one of the donkey's hind hooves, I felt it lurch forward and Yiannis grabbed the donkeys head collar. I know Cypriots can be very vocal when they get excited, even in jokey banter, but this shouting didn't seem friendly to me. I found out Yiannis had threatened to report these two to the ministry for neglect. When they heard this, they decided to leave without warning me first. I was still holding the hind leg up when they tried to walk off with the donkey.

A week or so later, one of the villagers contacted the sanctuary because they were worried for this donkey's welfare. So Yiannis contacted the ministry and with one of their staff and John, who drove the horsebox, the three of them went to confiscate this poor animal. They arrived at the women's home but they didn't answer the door. One of the locals told them that the women had hid the donkey but he knew where it was and took them to where it was hidden. The poor thing had to be carried into the horsebox and it was decided nothing could be done for it and it was put to sleep. It amazes me how some can be so cruel.

OUR DOGS AND STANLEY

I think anybody who reads about my life can see that both Phyl and I have had a love of dogs for many years. I know this hasn't got anything to do with shoeing horses but if you are writing your own book, you can write what the hell you want.

For over 50 years I have always had a dog or sometimes two dogs. Every dog that came into my life was from either a dog rescue sanctuary or, in Ally's case, the owner didn't want her anymore. Although I have owned many dogs before, I will start with Ally and Ben as we took both dogs with us when we moved to Cyprus. To me it didn't matter that a few of my dogs, over the years, may have included a few mongrels but I can assure you they always had a happy face. I treated them all the same and to me they were worth more to me than a Crufts pedigree winner. In my eyes, all our dogs were equals. I never wanted them to be a show dog or work dog. All I wanted was them to be a valued family member and enjoy their life.

Ally, a black Labrador bitch, came into my life when I was still working in the UK. She had been handed in at the local vets practice in Sileby were I lived at the time. I can still remember that Saturday morning as if it was yesterday, even though it was back in 1995. Ally came into my life when I had an appointment at the local vets for a remedial shoeing on a horse with a foot problem. Before I had got my kit out of my van, Bridget, who was a senior vet nurse at the time, said to me, 'Mick, come and have a look at this dog, folk keep handing her into us after catching her running loose in the street. She will be good for you.'

At the time I had just lost Holly, a little collie who went everywhere with me. I often thought Holly was going to live forever but she passed away when she was near 20 years old. Also, at the time, my first marriage had come to an end after a not nice divorce. My two sons still lived with me and my daughter not too far away. I often felt the house felt too quiet without a dog. Bridget knew I loved my dogs and thought this stray would have a good home with me. Mind you, I was a bit surprised when I saw Ally, a three-year-old Labrador bitch who stared at me as if to say, *we can be big mates*. Ally was nothing like I was expecting. I thought this stray dog was going to be a scruffy mongrel that was allowed to run wild until they had got caught by the dog warden, although that wouldn't have put me off. Bridget told me that she knew who owned Ally and she had taken her back to her home on numerous occasions. Locals had often took her into the vets when she was found wandering around the streets on her own. This last time Bridget took her back to her home, Ally's old owners told her that they didn't want her. They described her as a big pain in the neck.

'In what way?' I asked.

'They said she barks all day and when the shed door is opened, Ally shoots past them and down the road,' replied Bridget.

'Don't tell me that she was locked up in the shed all day? If she was, I can understand why she barks all of the time. As for when the door is finally opened, I can see why she wanted to run away. I would have done the same and you can't blame her for that,' I muttered.

'Well, Mick, if you don't want her the animal rescue folk are coming to collect her this afternoon,' Bridget said.

I had had to make my mind up rather quickly when I heard that animal rescue were coming for her. I must have given it a lot of thought for all of five seconds. So, yes, you can guess when I got the remedial work done on the horse, I left with Ally sitting in the passenger seat of my van.

Although I had a few issues with Ally in the first couple of months, she soon settled down and became a very faithful friend to me, as I was to her. I can remember shoeing a horse that was OK on its front feet but could be unpredictable on its hinds. Usually someone would hold onto the head collar while I shod its hind feet. That day though I had started before anyone had come to help and the vibes felt good from the first touch. Other farriers may agree that we can often sense what the behaviour of a horse is as soon as we start. That day, I got the front shoes on without too much bother without anybody helping me. I thought I will give the horse the benefit of the doubt and picked a hind foot up and nothing happened. I had got the old shoe off and started to foot trim when one of the girls said, 'I see you don't want me to help as Ally is doing a great job.'

I had noticed while I was working on the hind hoof the horse seemed to be leaning forward with its head down. I just thought that, although it wasn't the best working position for me, I didn't want to upset it to make it stand with its head up. When the young lady said Ally was helping, I looked behind me to see the horse with its head down and Ally licking the horse between its eyes. Over the years she seemed to know the ins and outs of the different stable yards. At this one it was as if she knew that horse could sometimes be a pain on the hind hooves.

Another time, I was shoeing at stables when another horse broke loose (not the one I was shoeing). All I heard was somebody shout and a horse galloping past me and heading to the open gate, which, if it turned right, it could have got onto the main road. If it turned left, it was not as bad as the road was more rural with grass growing down the middle, but even so the horse could have covered miles. Quick as a flash, Ally didn't go after the horse she ran under a post and rail fence and managed to turn the animal back into the stable yard. I was so proud of her. If she had chased the horse, it would have just took off out of the gate and God knows what could have happened.

I could write forever about my dogs and even if Ally had been a scruffy mongrel in the vets that Saturday morning, I would have still treated her the same.

I must say that Ally had one issue she never grew out of, which was if another dog came to visit us at our house. It was only at home she was fussy and wouldn't entertain any strange dog setting foot onto our yard, let alone the house. At stable yards or just out for a walk, it was fine if we met other pooches and she would be best of friends. She, however, accepted and seemed comfortable with Ben, a three-year-old saluki. Ally met Ben when I met Phyl, who later became my wife. The first time the dogs met each other was sitting on the back seat of my nearly-new car. We had gone out for the day with both dogs and we were a bit apprehensive about a dog fight. Well, nothing happened. Even when we had to leave them in the car for ten minutes. I was quite prepared that my car may not be in the nice condition we had left it in when we returned due to two scrapping dogs. Well, my worry disappeared when I saw two dogs sitting next to each other, waiting patiently for our return. It felt as if Ally had said to Ben, *well, Ben, they look to be couple now, so it is you and me now.*

Those two dogs stayed the best of mates until we lost first Ally aged 14. She had started to have problems going to the loo and looked to be in discomfort. We had by then moved to Cyprus. Yiannis, the vet I had got to know through working at the donkey sanctuary, had diagnosed cancer of the spleen after he had done several blood tests and X-rays. He had tried his best but with the best will in the world, the cancer had already started to spread. Also, the twinkle in her eyes had gone and we decided it was best not to put her through more pain. I can say this is something I have never found easy. It felt like by putting her to sleep I was murdering her. I kept somehow having to justify my decision and hated the day when Yiannis had to put Ally to sleep. Both Phyl and I stayed with her. She was on Yiannis's examination table when he first put her on a drip to sedate her. While she was on the drip, both of us were either side of her and as she got drowsy she pressed her face into my face for a second or two. Then she did the same to Phyl. Then back to me and then back to Phyl again. I am sure it was her way of saying goodbye. When she did go under, Yannis gave the injection to stop her heart and to be quite honest it felt she had left this world a happy dog.

I felt sorry for Ben because when I first met him, he would cower away from any adult man and that included me. I can remember the first few times I took both dogs for a walk I had to catch Ben in a rugby tackle on several occasions. It didn't take him long to realise I was no threat. With him being on the timid side, and Ally the more adventurous one, she seemed to bring him out of his shell. On the other hand, he seemed to have a more calming influence on her. Both dogs seemed to know they were good for each other.

I can remember a time Ally had gone into the sea for a swim when we were still living in the UK and on holiday in Anglesey in North Wales. The tide was coming in fast and she was struggling with the force of the pounding waves and began to panic. She managed to get herself onto a rock that was just about still sticking out of the sea and only seemed a few yards away from the beach. Nick, my youngest son, who was with us was going to go and get her. I thought that it wasn't a good idea as the last thing I would have wanted was for him to be swept out to the sea. We were all shouting at Ally to swim towards us. Ben had other ideas, he kept running into the sea up to his chest and kept barking at Ally then running out, then back in again and barking as if to say, *swim to me*. Eventually, after what felt like an age but I suppose it was only minutes, she did just that and jumped off the rock and managed to swim towards him. He never stopped barking until she had got to him and both were out of the water.

Over the years those two dogs were the best of mates. No dog fights although it was plain to see that Ally was boss. I say boss, unless it was dinner time then he was boss and didn't she know it. As I say, they didn't fight but had their little ways by looks and little growls. Ally being a Labrador scoffed her food down as if there was no tomorrow. Ben would take his time and sometimes he wouldn't eat all his dinner. Ally always stood nearby just in case. He wouldn't allow her to interfere while he was eating but if he had finished and had left any, he would only then let her finish it off.

One day I watched her as she scoffed her dinner down in record time. When she finished eating, she stood two paces away from Ben. Her head tilted slightly pretending as if she was looking away from Ben's dinner, but I could see her eyes were firmly fixed on how much he was going to leave. I knew she was hoping he was going to leave some and he would let her have what was left but not until he had had enough. There was a bit of a clatter as if something had fallen off a shelf in the living room and Ben left his dinner to investigate. After what must have only been only a second or two, he came back just as Ally was about to stick her head into his food bowl. Quick as a flash she stood back and with her head tilted to one side, pretended to be looking in the other direction from Ben. To me watching, I had to laugh as it stuck out like a sore thumb what Ally was thinking. Although her head was facing one way, her eyes were still firmly fixed on Ben's food bowl with a look that said, *I wasn't going to eat it, honest!*

Having lost Ally to cancer, we couldn't believe that Ben started to be a bit lame on one of his hind legs and that turned out to be a cancer too. Although he never showed too much emotion, I am sure it hit him hard when Ally died and he had looked a bit lost without her. With Ben we had started using another vet who was a lot nearer to us than Yiannis – nothing to do with his treatments. It was an hour's journey to him and ten minutes to this other one. What we didn't know and found out later was the drugs she gave us to slow Ben's cancer down was actually doing the opposite and speeding up Ben's death. Everything Ben ate after starting this treatment caused him to cry out in pain afterwards. That should have been alarm bells for us because that dog never once complained, even when he went lame. That is perhaps easier to see now as, at the time, we were more concerned about his comfort. We assumed the cancer had started to spread. It was only days later we thought we couldn't be having him suffering like that and the best thing was to put him to sleep.

When we lost Ben, I was certain I didn't want another dog. I am sure I am not alone and like other pet owners who get upset as I do when we lose a best friend. It is not the looking after bit that bothers me, it's losing them at the end of their life. I can even understand folk clinging onto their pet's life longer than they should. Everybody sometimes prays for a miracle, but that miracle rarely comes. Many times I have said never again, and a few months later I get withdrawal symptoms from not having a dog's company.

I have got to mention Stanley who had turned up as a stray dog at the donkey sanctuary. At the time there was a husband and wife and their male friend who all came from Sri Lanka and worked as grooms. When Stanley walked into the sanctuary, the grooms instantly took to him, and it didn't take too long before he was living with them. Every day they would bring him to work and soon he became part of the sanctuary. I often thought with the attention he got from the tourists who visited, he could get many donations like the donkeys got for adoption.

Two or three years after I had started as the donkey sanctuary farrier, there was a change in management. One of the other changes was a new home had to be found for Stanley as the Sri Lankan's where returning to their homeland. Our friends, John and Gill, were the ones who gave him his new home. Gill, who has a heart of gold where animals are concerned and worked at the sanctuary, volunteered to give Stanley his new home. John, on the other hand, was not sure. Although their home was in Paphos and the donkey sanctuary an hour's drive away, Gill lived nearby to her work and only came home on weekends. That meant John would be looking after Stanley during the week and he was the one who was not sure about having a dog. Well, I think Stanley became John's soulmate. He took him everywhere with him. If John called in at our house, Stanley would be with him.

Before they took Stanley on, sometimes John would give a helping hand if the sanctuary had a staff shortage. He often left his motor with the doors and windows wide open to help to keep it cool. Stanley would see this as an invitation to make himself comfortable on the back seat. I laugh about it now. When John saw Stanley curled up comfortably on the back seat, we would hear him shouting, 'Get the hell out, I don't want blooming dog hairs over the seats!' Or words with a bit more essence in the sentence.

MICK O'REARDON

How things changed when Stanley and John became quite attached to each other. I think he found having a dog around the house good company. He took him for walks early in the morning and early evenings when the sun was not up to its searing heat. Sometimes, John would already be at the sanctuary and would have taken Stanley with him. I can remember one day when I arrived, I had got out of my motor and walked past John's motor, not realising Stanley was laid on the backseat. I must have only gone two paces past when I heard a dog talking in a doggy language, but not in an aggressive way. I looked behind and saw Stanley's head poking out of the back window as if to say, well, *are you not speaking to me today?* I had to go and pat him on the head and say hello to him. Again, he seemed to talk back to me in his doggy language. He was such a character and any person who loved dogs would have adored him.

I had to laugh another day when I heard John talking to Stanley again laid flat out on the backseat of his motor. Remember, only a few months before, Stanley wasn't allowed to set foot in his motor. This time he had left the doors open and I heard John talking in a soft, caring voice. 'Are you all right, babe, I will put a blanket over the window so you are in the shade, you are not too hot are you?' Now he was asking Stanley if he was comfortable. The dog hairs didn't seem to matter anymore.

Stanley had one thing that he hated and that was Yiannis the vet. If the Sanctuary had booked a vet appointment they always knew when Yiannis was five minutes away when Stanley was there. We could be having a coffee break and Stanley would give out one or two growls and grumbles and everybody would say,

'Yiannis is nearly here.' A few minutes later, with the grumbles getting louder, the vet would arrive.

I can remember another occasion when I was with John and Stanley. We had stopped for a beer on the way home after trimming the donkeys' hooves. It was at a taverna in a village called Avdimou. We must have been there 20 minutes or so when Stanley suddenly started to get a bit excited with his usual grumbles when there was something he was not sure about. We thought maybe it was how the locals were in deep conversation discussing something or another in loud excitable voices, as if all hell was about to break loose. Both John and myself, over the years, had got used to locals talking as if there was no tomorrow. I found out over the years this shouting chat was not as bad as it may seem. Mind you, a few years before I once thought the same when I first heard what sounded as if all hell could happen any minute. When I asked the bar owner what the argument was about, he roared with laughter and said, 'Argument? They are not arguing, they are on about how well one of the guy's sitting room got decorated.'

We both thought, *what's upset Stanley?* It couldn't be these guys shouting in excitable voices as they had been very vocal since we had arrived. Stanley surely would have heard it all before. Five minutes later, Stanley got more agitated when a vehicle went past. We couldn't believe it, it was Yiannis the vet. That dog must have had blooming good hearing, or could he sniff him out from when he was miles away.

John and Gill asked me if Phyl and I would mind looking after Stanley as they were going back to the UK for a week's holiday. We had not had a dog for a while then. It was after Ben had died we had started to miss having a dog around the house and we were more than happy to look after him. We both thought it was better than him stuck in boarding kennels. After all, he was now used to all the mod cons that John and Gill provided him with. I think Stanley thought he had trained John and Gill to his house rules and not theirs. It is exactly the same at our home as sometimes I think we go by the dog's rules in our house too.

John had often dropped in at our home in Koili and he always had Stanley with him, so Stan knew our home quite well. We knew we would enjoy his company and taking him for walks in the early mornings and in the evenings when the hot summer days were a little cooler. Both Phyl and I often thought, *we are not the boss in our house again, where Stanley was concerned*. We seemed to be living by his rules. All our dogs we have ever had seemed to know we could be a soft touch to get their way and Stanley soon had us wrapped around his little paw. He soon sussed us out too. He liked to be comfortable and soon wangled his way into our bedroom which was the coolest room in the house. Gill had warned us and had brought a blanket to cover our bed just in case. We found out he had trained John and Gill well and would often be found laid flat out on their bed too. When Stanley came back from his morning walk and the sun was getting too hot outdoors, he would make straight for our bedroom. Mind you, we found it quite amusing how he would lay there, then raise his head and look up at the ceiling fan above as if to say, *I could do with that on too.*

I have a sign on our living room wall and I think it may have been written by a dog as I am told by lots of dog owners that they believe it to be so true.

Dog Rules
1 *Got a dog*
2 *Dog sleeps in garage*
3 *OK, dog can be in the house,*
   But not on the sofa.
4 *OK, dog can be on the sofa,*
   But not on the bed.
5 *OK, dog can be on the bed,*
   But not under the covers.
6 *I think we will have to get the dog's permission*
   To get into bed.

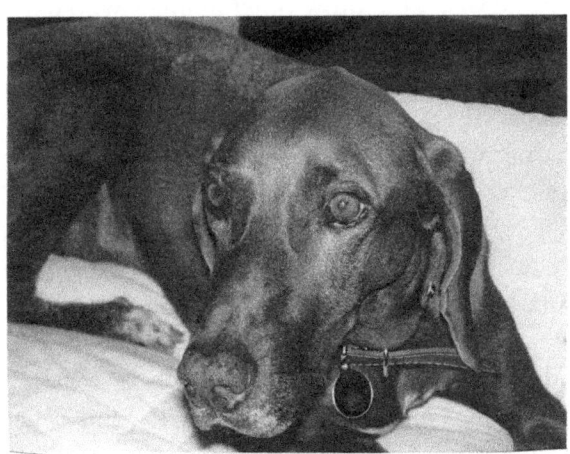

Stanley.

JACK

Just over a year after losing Ben, Jack, our lovely bearded collie, had come to live with us after his old owners couldn't look after him anymore. Jack was no stranger to us as we had met him several times before we took him on. He was a friendly and faithful dog to us and it felt he had lived with us all his life. Now we had Jack, would he accept Stanley, and vice versa. We had found Jack to be very friendly with humans, but, like Ally, he wouldn't allow other animals who dared to enter our garden. He felt he had to protect us. He had only lived with us for a few months and we had got used to his little ways. What would happen if Stanley was to stay when John and Gill wanted to go on their holidays, or would he have to be found boarding kennels. Sure enough, we did get asked and we thought worst case scenario we may have to just keep the two dogs apart somehow if they didn't like each other. The first time they met each other, to our relief, they liked each other and ended up becoming the best of mates. As time went by, Jack even got excited if John called in with Stanley and the same if we visited their house, and it was no problem for them to look after Jack either.

Two or three years later, Stanley didn't look very well after having treatment on his teeth. John and Gill had taken him to the same vet we had taken Ben to. Again, it was nearer than Yiannis, who Stanley was not too keen on (mind you, the only thing he had ever had done to him was a needle stuck in him for his yearly injection).

What we learnt later was if a dog is to have treatment on their teeth, especially an older dog, it is best to give antibiotics and feed them a dollop of yoghurt for a few days afterwards. This helps to kill any bad bacteria swallowed from what comes off their teeth. From what we can gather, poor Stanley had neither and ended up with stomach trouble. The vet then prescribed anti-inflammatory and steroids. We had called in at John and Gill's and to see Stanley laying on their settee and he didn't look at all well. This friendly and sometimes mischievous dog didn't look like the Stanley we knew. Jack seemed to sense this too. He stood near him, tilting his head one way then another at Stanley as if to say, *I wish I could make you better.*

At the donkey sanctuary Yiannis asked Gill how Stanley was, knowing and understanding why they had used a vet closer to home. She told him what he had been prescribed and when he heard the dosage of the steroids, his eyes opened really wide and he said, 'Don't give Stanley that. That dosage would be too much for a donkey, let alone a dog. It will be like exploding his stomach.'

That warning came too late. John had already been giving it to him for several days and the poor dog was deteriorating fast and needed veterinary care. This time they rushed Stanley over to Yiannis and the poor dog didn't grumble once at him. He hadn't got the energy to kick up a fuss. The sad thing was nothing could be done for him although for a few more days they did hope for a miracle like most of us dog lovers do.

A few days after Stanley died, we called in with Jack at Gill and John's. I know Stanley in general was not a noisy dog, but their house was too quiet. Jack seemed to sense this and went searching their house, looking for his best friend. I think he already knew he wasn't going to find him and started whimpering like a human does in sad circumstances.

The other sad thing, although we didn't realise it at the time, was when Ben died, he had been prescribed the same medication as Stanley. It was only when Yiannis told Gill that we realised that is what had happened to Ben. When he ate anything, he cried out in pain and he was a dog who never showed pain. After that, we travelled the extra miles to Yiannis's surgery with Jack.

ODE TO JACK
2001–2018 AGED 17

You came into our life
In such a plight
Evicted out of home
Worried where to spend the night

Your big brown eyes
Is what we saw
You told no lies
No trouble for the law

With love and friendship
You soon had us trained
Panting like a steamship
Is the one way you explained?

We were like doubles
Oh, what a friend you are
Listening to our troubles
Especially when out in the car

The darkest days have come
We can see you are not well
You don't look at home
It's in your eyes that tell

No more running in the park
With windswept hair in the breeze
Letting out an excited bark
Yes, you did like to tease

Mick O'Reardon 2019

Our gorgeous Jack.

ART

Phyl had always wanted to take up painting in retirement. She had done a little years before but with bringing up a family and work she never could find the time. When we saw an open evening at Nik Costa's art studio in Paphos, we thought we would see what was on offer. Nik had pictures on show what some of his students had done and was advertising he had places in three art classes. Beginners, improvers and advanced. Phyl decided to join the improvers class and Nik said, 'What about you, Mick, do you want to join too?'

'What about me, I can't draw to save my life. The only art I have done is when I made scrolls when I did any wrought iron work. I was never good with a paint brush even for decorating the house. The only thing I was good at was painting windows but not very good on the window frames.'

Nik must have convinced me because I joined the art class too and surprised myself with what I could achieve. OK, I was not on the same level as Phyl, although I found that some of my paintings and drawings were masterpieces to me. I think other folk may have a different opinion though. I must confess that while I didn't set out to paint an abstract it may have ended up looking like one when I had finished.

Nik would give us different drawing and painting exercises every week. One or two of my attempts I would have considered as not bad for me, although I don't think the Louvre would have had an interest. Then again, I don't think my living room wall would have entertained them either.

On other occasions, Nik would organise a model for life drawing classes. The first life drawing class I attended was in winter so the model who was posing starkers needed to be kept warm. Nik had heaters blasting out warm that to me was like sitting in a sauna. After she had been posing in one position for a while, I felt my artistic licence was not enhancing her body. No matter how I tried, I made this poor lady's body look more like a character out of a cartoon. Then disaster struck. The poor women fainted right in front of me. Two or three of us rushed to her aid and after having a drink of water, she recovered. It was decided for the rest of the lesson to have her in a different pose, laid on a sun lounger and the heating was turned down a touch as she said the heat had got to her. I thought, *thank God she hasn't seen my drawing of her as she may have fainted again.*

In the second life drawing class a different lady was the model. I found that while I was drawing her, she was just an object rather than a person. My focus was getting an arm clutching a leg right, or trying to alter a nose I had got too big and so forth. I found, although the models were naked, I never really noticed this as my only focus was getting body proportions right. This second life drawing class was not the same as the first one, although the model didn't faint on us. She did things differently. We always stopped for a break and the models would put a dressing gown on and come and admire our attempts. This lady, though, didn't bother. She strode around the room, looking at the artwork on show, *naked*. She chatted with all the artists in turn, which included me. Let me say it was hard to look at her in the eye while she spoke. I didn't know if I should be looking at the ceiling, the floor or her body—no, I mean her face.

After six months or so, Nik suggested I may be better at sculpture than painting. I had never thought I was cut out to do art or sculpture, but I surprised myself at sculpture even though I had made fancy scroll work in my early blacksmithing days.

My first task was to chisel a dog's head out of a bit of rock. This sits as an ornament still to this day in our garden. Then I welded a load of scrap metal together that consisted of rods used to reinforce concrete, a radiator that came out of an old fridge and other scrap I found on rubbish dumps. This heap of scrap metal became what other students called Metal Micky. The sculpture was of a guy who resembled a cross between Worzel Gummidge and a tramp. I had created a bowler hat and a jacket with a tail as if he had at one time worked as a butler. I had him stood slightly forward as if he was greeting someone with his arm slightly raising his hat. I was amazed some other arty folk took an interest in Metal Micky and sent a picture of him to their friends all over the globe. I think he still stands proudly outside Nik's studio, greeting his students. As for me learning sculpture, I got a bit confused though. I had a little arc welder and sometimes thought was it me learning the art of sculpture or was it me teaching welding as I was the only one who could?

Phyl, though, only a couple of years later had her paintings on display at various locations and even sold many and even got commissions. One painting was of me shoeing a horse in Northern Cyprus. (The front cover on this book.) She also got to know well known artists throughout Cyprus and had a studio of her own.

WROUGHT IRON FENCE

I had taken my farrier tools to Cyprus which included the gas forge that I had used from the back of my van to heat up horseshoes. I hadn't intended the forge for shoeing horses but to build a wrought iron fence at the back of our Cypriot home. Before it was just open, and though other houses had built little wooden fences, we wanted something different. I found a steel stockist and got my steel delivered and set to work constructing my fence. A few years earlier, I had made what is known as a scroll tool which helped in making scrolls when I did work on my home in the UK. This came in handy again and in no time I got my wrought iron fence constructed. The trouble was that neighbours then asked if I could do little welding jobs for them. It ranged from repairing rotting railings leading up steps to their houses to making garden gates, and many other welding jobs.

Nik, the art teacher, asked if I could build steel railings around the flat roof of a chalet he let out to artists on holiday in the garden at his home. It had a roof terrace and had no barrier to stop folk falling off the edge. I decided it was best to construct on site. There was plenty of room on the flat roof so I had all my gear and steel that the steel stockist had delivered lifted up. Nick, my youngest son, who was staying with us at the time, would give me a hand. Nik didn't want anything fancy, so I didn't need to do any scroll work.

I got Nick to cut the upright bars ready for me to weld into a frame for the railings. Cyprus was so hot in summer that Nick and I would be at Nik's at six in the morning. By 11am the temperature would be scorching and we would call it a day. I can remember one very hot morning when the sun was already scorching by 10:30am. Nick was cutting the steel to length and I would pick them up to weld into the frame of the fence and found some didn't fit. They were too long. I said, 'Nick, they are not fitting, has the measuring stop moved?' (This was a gig we had rigged up to save measuring with the tape measure every time we needed several lengths the same length). He was about to take a sliver off when I said, 'Oh, leave it, Nick, do it in the morning. Let's call it a day, it's getting too hot up here.'

Next morning, when the air was cooler, all the bars of steel fitted perfectly without Nick needing to cut anything off. He had been cutting them at the right length and because they were laid in the hot sun the steel expanded like a railway line does.

When we were nearly finished, Nik asked if I could build a gazebo. Again with my son's help, we got that built too. It stood proudly in the middle of the roof terrace.

After I got Nik's fence and gazebo erected, some of his friends who I will call Pete and Anna asked me if I could build railings leading up steps to the flat roof of their home. Pete was English and Anna was Dutch, and a top actress in the Netherlands. They had a guy who had constructed a very bad attempt with wood. It was so loose I never had to unscrew anything. All I did was give it a good shove and it more or less fell over. That is how unsecure it was. If someone had lent hard on it they could have fallen from a great height. So that was another job I got without asking. Again, they didn't want anything too fancy and three or four days later, with the help of my son, we got the railings built. Anna remarked that if our effort fell down, it would bring the house down too.

Railings I built.

OLD LADY'S DONKEY

A few weeks went by when I got a phone call from Anna one evening. My first thought was, *don't tell me the railings have fallen down*, but was relieved when she asked if I would look at an old lady's donkey. She lived in the same village as her and said the donkey was struggling to walk. Various old guys had given it a variety of lotions and potions but to no avail. With how Anna described the problem, I thought the medication administered could be given until it came out of the donkeys ears and it would still be lame. So next morning, Phyl and I met up with Anna as her Greek was better than mine and we went to see if I could get this lady's donkey better. As I have said, lots of the old folk have their money tied up in land and had limited cash, so they would barter with produce as payment. I had a good idea this call was going to be one where money wouldn't be involved.

Again, I had a good idea what the problem could be and Anna took us to the lady's home, which looked as if it needed a full refurbishment. By the state of it, I don't think it ever had one since the place was built in the year dot. Anyway, the old gal looked me up and down a few times as if she was sussing me out. It felt like she was deciding if she could trust me to treat her donkey. She spoke to Anna very fast as if she had a time limit to get the words out of her mouth, and so loud most the village could hear. I thought, *she doesn't trust me.* What did I know about making lame donkeys better? Anna, I suppose, spoke in broken Greek back to her and I thought she was trying to reassure her I was a qualified farrier. I was wrong – she was pleased to see me. The old gal had asked Anna if I was a doctor, meaning a vet. As I say, Anna was not fluent with the language and didn't know the Greek term for a farrier and told the old gal, 'Yes he is a doctor.' I then became Doctor Mick.

So Doctor Mick got led to the patient standing tied to a tree stump in the paddock. It was not hard to spot which foot was the problem as the donkey was standing on three legs and holding up its near fore and pointing the hoof. It didn't take me long to find a very ripe abscess. I asked Anna if the lady had any bran as I wanted to put a poultice on to help to draw the infection. I had got a good idea she wouldn't have an Animalintex poultice or even heard of one. Luckily, she did have some bran and I asked on the off chance if she had some Epsom salts and as a bonus she got that too. I used to mix the Epsom salts with the bran but I wouldn't have worried too much if she didn't have any. Anna watched what I did as she would go and change it the next day and I would visit the animal four days later. I placed the donkey's foot into a plastic feed bag which the poultice was made in. I had to improvise with duct tape to fasten it to the donkey's hoof as I didn't have any vet wrap bandages.

The lady was so pleased I found what the problem was, and she talked to me in very loud Greek, with a bit of sign language of her holding a glass to her lips and drinking. I understood her perfectly as, although these folk don't have much money, they do barter with vegetables and often haloumi, but I never imagined I would get paid with alcohol. Yes, what she was asking was, did I drink Zivania. When I heard the word "Zivania", I raised my thumb to indicate I did.

Well, this drink is made from distilled fermented grape skins. Supermarkets sell a weak version of it but if it is produced in some homemade village distillery it is more like rocket fuel. After one small measure you feel you need the fire brigade to put the fire out inside your mouth, throat and stomach. Plus, it instantly makes your voice husky for a few minutes after. Saying that, this moonshine got rid of a yellow stain in our bath which other cleaning substances hadn't touched. Good for cleaning windows too. A friend who was visiting us got a prickly heat rash and rubbed this "cleaning fluid" into her skin and it worked when all other lotions had failed. Another guy we knew had an operation on his leg but the wound wouldn't heal. After various lotions and potions had no effect, he rubbed zivania into the wound and a couple of days later the wound had started to heal. We found out if the Cypriots had any ailments or sickness, they used zivania as a form of medicine.

So when I told this lady I liked a drink, I got an idea this was going to be part of my payment. She disappeared into her home and after a few minutes she appeared carrying a cardboard box full of mushrooms, cabbages, carrots, haloumi and two bottles – one a plastic milk bottle and the other a 7 Up fizzy drink bottle – full to the brim with liquid that must have been similar to rocket fuel. By Jove, was that potent and I still had a bottle of it 11 years later.

Old Lady's lame donkey.

WROUGHT IRON WORK,
A WELL-PAID HOBBY

I started to wonder had I retired or was this wrought iron work and welding jobs my idea of a hobby? Well, if it was a hobby I was getting paid well to do it. After constructing Nik's gazebo and railings and Anna and Pete's stair banister railings, another couple asked me to make railings near their swimming pool. They were worried that one day a car could easily end up in the pool of their holiday home. They often had people who rented off them when they were not in the country. The driveway was in line with their swimming pool and they had visions that holiday makers arriving on a dark night could end up parking their rented car in the swimming pool. This job only took me a morning to make and an hour to fix and I wondered how long before the next. I had only lived in Cyprus a short while, intending to retire. I had never asked anyone for work, work seemed to be running after me.

Bob and Margaret, our friends, wanted a garden gate making plus they got me to reinforce the metal work that supported bamboo panels to give their garden a bit more privacy. The framework was only a single frame with the bamboo panels tied to it. Every time there was a strong breeze the bamboo panels would break loose.

I suggested building another frame with the panels sandwiched between the two. I am pleased to say my idea worked as they never had any more issues with any windy weather.

At Charles and Barbara's house, their garden gate was a steel frame balanced across the entrance. I had often heard Barbara moan about having the performance to lift it to enter and leave their house. The only reason they had it as a barrier was to stop their dog escaping.

It was while they were away on holiday I decided to change this iron frame into a gate. Barbara's parents were staying to look after the dog when I mentioned to her dad about building a proper gate. Would they mind? He thought she would be grateful.

It didn't take too long, and was not hard, for me to get the steel frame made into a gate that opened and closed on hinges. I told the father not to mention it if they got in touch while they were away. We would wait until they came home and see if they noticed it was easier to enter their garden.

The day came for their return and we were sitting outside on our balcony. We watched Barbara get out of the car and open the gate and then she twigged that she opened a gate on hinges and shouted, 'Ooh, the gate fairy has been!'

Next door to Charles and Barbara, at Bill and Norma's, they had a gate at the side of their house that led into their garden. Between the gate and the fence separating them from next door, it was open. So anyone could just walk on the garden and around the gate. They asked me if I could build a wrought iron fence to make their garden more private.

It was a quite straightforward job and I was getting on fine. Bill kept me supplied with tea and held anything that needed holding while I welded. I wasn't far off finished when Bill said they had to go out. They hadn't been gone long when disaster struck. I was cutting a piece of steel when the cutting disc broke. The broken bit hit me in the face and in seconds there was blood everywhere. My first thought was to grab a rag, a very dirty rag at that, to stem the blood. At this stage, I had no idea what damage there was to my face but our house was nearby and I thought I needed to get home quick.

Once I reached home, I think I said to Phyl, 'Please don't faint on me,' when she saw me covered in blood. Luckily, she didn't and was horrified to see a deep gash in my face and said I needed to go to the hospital.

My reaction was, 'No, I will be fine. When I take the rag away from my face can you wash the wound? I am sure a sticking plaster will be OK.'

Well, she didn't faint on me and got me cleaned up. Unfortunately, we hadn't got any plasters big enough. So while Phyl went off to buy plasters and antiseptic ointments, I was left at home holding a clean towel over the gash in my face which was still trying its best to bleed. When Phyl returned and got me patched up, she still thought I ought to go to the hospital as I may need a few stiches. I must confess I did have a peek in the mirror while Phyl was out buying plasters. I must say I was horrified by how bad it looked. It did give me a bit of concern but I tried to convince Phyl I would be fine and went and finished Bill and Norma's fence. I didn't go to the hospital but my wound healed up without any trace of a scar.

CHARLES AND BARBARA'S RESTAURANT

I have mentioned how Phyl had been asked by Barbara and Charles to help out for one night only at the opening of their restaurant. She thought it was to do a bit of washing up but two years later she was still there, and never did any washing up. She ended up serving meals to the diners. Sometimes she would ring me and ask if I would do the bar if they were having a busy night. It saved time for the waitresses if they didn't have to serve the drinks. If a table of eight ordered eight different drinks it took a great amount of time to organise. So with me serving the refreshments, it meant no food had got cold before it reached the table.

One Christmas day, Charles asked me if I would like to do the bar and greet the diners with a glass of Prosecco before they were shown to their table. Well that sounded easy enough but I felt a fool when I couldn't get the top off the first bottle. I know that you hold the top and turn the bottle, but this bottle cork refused to budge. I always thought I had a good grip after years of clinging onto awkward horses but this bottle of Prosecco was definitely making me look a fool. Then one diner said, 'Oh, give it here, let's have ago.'

I was praying he couldn't get the top off either, more so I didn't look the only fool, and guess what, he couldn't. I decided to get another one that had been put in the freezer to make sure it were chilled, and again the next one was the same. I know alcohol doesn't freeze but these blooming bottle corks seemed to be frozen on. I had now a queue of people waiting and somehow my mind went into overdrive to think of a solution. I thought of my grandmother. If she couldn't open a tight bottle or jar, she would wedge it between the door frame and door while she turned the bottle or jar. Luckily my grandmother's remedy worked to a huge cheer. So every bottle of Prosecco I had to open I had to stick in the door frame. After that, the diners got served their Christmas dinners without any further problems. If anything, the frozen corks had created a bit of amusement.

When the last guests had left, Charles and Barbara had insisted all the staff have Christmas dinner with them. With us on our own, we thought it was wonderful as we had not had to buy or cook our Christmas dinner at home. Another lady who was a waitress and lived on her own had thought the same as us too. I had never imagined that me of all people would be helping in a fine dining restaurant on a Christmas day. I don't mind eating good food but serving it was something I would not to be classed as a professional at doing. The other bonus was two tables had ordered a bottle of champagne that lunchtime and had only drunk less than half the bottle each so we made sure the rest didn't go to waste.

On the New Year's Eve, Charles asked me again if I could help him in the restaurant kitchen, helping him prepare dishes as Barbara wanted to be in the front of the house. I knew I could cook a good fry up but this was fine dining. I thought if he expected me to cook any exotic dishes that were on the menu they may be not classed as fine dining when it was served to the customer if I was the chef. I know I liked eating fine food but my cooking was more of a Greasy Joe's establishment in some roadside layby. Then again, Greasy Joe's place may look like fine dining against mine.

Anyway, Charles convinced me I would be fine and I was in the kitchen with a chef's hat on. I thought I looked like a chef even if I hadn't got a clue what I was doing. I found I only had to chop up carrots and parsnips. Put food on plates, but it had to be placed on nicely not like how I pile it on for my own dinners. Some roasted potatoes were done a little too well for Charles's liking and he said to throw them away. I knew the staff were going to eat later so I put these well-done spuds to one side. They were nice and crunchy, just how I like them. Mind you, another minute roasting I would have barbecued them. When the evening finished and guests were leaving, many came to me and thanked me for the superb meal. I didn't have the heart to say I had never done anything like that in my life. I felt I was a professional chef even though Charles did most of the cooking.

Over two years we helped out Barbara and Charles loads of times and he would always insist on Sundays that Phyl had to bring a dinner home for me when I was not helping. As for Phyl, that one night to help them out lasted two years.

JOHN AND ME ON AN OUTREACH

On odd occasions it was just John and myself who went on outreaches, especially before Yiannis became the sanctuary's vet. Sometimes I was asked to be a vet as well as a farrier. I will never forget the day we attended to a donkey belonging to an old lady who lived in village deep in the Troodos Mountains. She used her donkey to collect rose petals which she sold to cosmetic companies. Her faithful friend had overgrown hooves and a touch of laminitis. The trouble was the length of the hooves needed me to go round two or three times each with my nippers. The old lady seemed a bit startled by how much overgrown hoof I was chopping off.

I know Cypriot people can talk very loud and fast and look as if to kill if they feel threatened. This lady was shouting and waving her arms about and I got the feeling she thought I was harming her precious donkey. If I heard an English person shouting and acting the same way, I would think that they were not too pleased with me. Although the big clue in that case would be I would know what they are saying and here I didn't. When I learned more Greek, I realised that is how they talk when they are excited.

That time, I wasn't sure if she thought I was butchering her donkey's feet as she was only two-foot away from me, flapping her arms and pointing and shouting as I trimmed her donkey. John hadn't got a clue if she was angry or pleased with us. He decided the best thing to do was to ring Maria, a Cypriot lady, who worked in the donkey sanctuary office and ask for her to explain what I was doing. He gave the old lady his phone and she still seemed to sound agitated to us while talking to Maria. Then I was handed the phone as Maria wanted to talk to me. The first thing I said was, 'She doesn't seem happy with me, Maria.'

'Mick, she thinks you are wonderful. She can't remember her donkey's feet looking that good. A guy in her village used to hack a bit off now and then but he used a saw.'

'Oh, that's a relief, Maria, I thought she thought I was killing her donkey,' I said and was relieved she liked what I was doing.

When we had finished, the old gal took us into her home, which was just four walls. It was a one-room house with one window. The furniture consisted of two double beds, a stove that looked as if it were new in 1930, a couple of cupboards and four chairs and a table. One of the beds looked as if it was used as her wardrobe as clothes were piled high on it. Other than that, the place was clean and tidy. We were offered a large mug of tea and a massive chunk of the tastiest apple sponge cake I had ever had.

It brought back memories of shoeing horses at farms in the 1960s before they were modernised. I can remember the hospitality when the horse was shod – the farmer and his wife would insist on a mug of tea and a slice of cake. I think of the times I entered the little farm kitchen and the aromas of a freshly baked cake would hit me. The farmer's wife would have prepared a brew in a pint mug ready to help wash down a very large portion of freshly baked cake. This lady's welcoming was how I remembered those little farms when I first started work.

When we left, I had to confess to John if she had offered another slice of cake I would have had a job not to refuse. He thought the same as me. As for her shouting while I trimmed her donkey, I found out it was the way the Cypriots talk. If at the time I had learnt a little more of the language I may have understood her better. We made several more visits over the years and we were greeted every time with a very friendly smile and tea and apple sponge cake when we had finished.

Another time I was with John we had a call near Larnaca from a guy who wanted us to trim a very long overdue donkey's hooves. We had heard the guy could be an awkward so-and-so and as soon as we met him both of us took an instant dislike to him. Also, the donkey in question could be a handful too and downright dangerous. Some of these Cypriot donkeys are a lot bigger and stronger than the ones in the UK and this one was massive. This chap also asked if we knew an English couple who were looking for somewhere to live as he had got a bungalow. I think he said an English couple because we were English. If he was talking to a Bulgarian or someone from another country, he would have asked if they knew a couple of their nationality. All he wanted in return was to help him on his land now and then. The more he spoke, the more I got the feeling the cottage was free if the occupants worked eight hours a day, every day, for him with no pay. He wasn't the normal poor villager trying to make ends meet but very wealthy. When he showed John and I this "bungalow" I thought it looked more like a place where his hens used to live. It was filthy and with no bathroom or running water. Also, we soon got the idea he may not want to pay us either. The donkey sanctuary rule was if folk were not hard up, they had to pay the going rate to the sanctuary. I know I got paid regardless by the sanctuary. I didn't like the idea that those who were wealthy took advantage of a freebee, and this guy was one who didn't want to pay.

As for the donkey in question, he was an oversexed Jack. In other words, a stallion that had covered every Jenny (female) he owned. He was moaning that he got too many donkeys but if this Jack donkey lived in the same paddock as the Jenny's, this breeding was unlikely to stop. We had heard from George Hourie to watch ourselves as this Jack could put up a good fight and by golly it did. It was one of the biggest and strongest donkeys that I had had to attend to. Much bigger than the ones in the UK.

As soon as we entered the barn where he was shut in, the first thing it did was to turn its backside on us and kick out with both back hooves and that was before we got a head collar on. The owner let us know that no way was he going to go in. He wasn't going to get his head kicked in and so he disappeared. So with two long ropes we managed to get the thing tied to a gate with the two ropes wrapped around its body and eventually a head collar on. George was right, we had got to watch ourselves because if it didn't get you with just its feet it could get you with its teeth too. We had to put another lead rope round its mouth to stop it biting.

I set around trimming its very long front hooves when a young guy appeared. He was a big strong lad and suggested getting another rope and trying to tie its hind leg up to the five-bar gate. That was easy seeing as it was the side against the gate, but how would I manage to trim? I needed space and no way could I squeeze between the donkey and the five-bar gate. Then the donkey solved that problem. It kicked out and got its hind hoof stuck and it happened to be sticking out on the other side of the gate. The chap who had arrived quickly tied its leg to the gate before it managed to free itself. It was in the perfect position for me and I climbed over the gate and soon had that overgrown hind foot trimmed. Now we had got one front foot done and a hind one done on the opposite side. Before we undid the hind leg from the gate, we had tied another rope around the other hind leg, ready to start its other two hooves. We needed to turn the thing round to tackle the other side. The front was not a problem but the hind was the more difficult one. Once the young guy pulled on the rope to hoist its leg up and it did the same thing again. It kicked out and got its other hind leg caught through the bars of the gate. I have shod many a wild horse in my time, but I have to say this stallion donkey topped the lot.

We got this donkey trimmed and when we left we were sure the owner would be pleased with us even though we had managed to charge him the going rate. That was until someone at the sanctuary had read an article in the local paper that he had written about the sanctuary. He hadn't got a nice word to say or any praise for what we had done and was surprised he had to pay the going rate... In other words, we were useless.

This chap ought to have put his brain into gear before he opened his mouth. He needed our services again a few months later. John and I went and we made it the last call of the day. One of his other donkeys was a bit lame, he told Marie at the office. When we saw the lame one, it was far from a bit lame. The poor thing couldn't stand. All four hooves were overgrown and it was suffering from chronic laminitis. The poor thing also had abscesses in both its front hooves. We did the best we could and advised the guy to call a vet. It needed to be put on bute (painkiller) right away and they also needed to get the stallion out of the enclosure it had to share with the Jenny. It was still trying to mount it and was kicking it to death. He said he hoped it to be in foal, we said we hoped it wasn't.

Anyway, he wasn't going to call the vet because of the expense. He would treat the donkey himself with aspirins. He would give it a couple as they worked for himself when he got a headache to get rid of pain. Aspirins wouldn't make this poor thing better, a lot stronger medical help was needed. These folk really annoy me. This guy had money coming out of his ears and would sooner let a defenceless animal suffer than part with a bit of his fortune. Perhaps we ought to have put an article in the local paper about him.

TAKEOVER

Two or three years after I started doing the donkeys
for Patrick and Mary, they decided that the sanctuary
was getting too much for them and another organisation
took over. I thought things may move in a direction I was
used to working in when I did my farrier work in the UK.
I understood that Mary and Patrick had no choice to run
the welfare of the donkeys on a shoestring which they did
brilliantly I must say. Now more money was going to be
available. Which in one way was good. I was not amused
though when I got lectures off some young kid who
wasn't a farrier who had flown to Cyprus from the UK to
tell me how to trim a donkey's hooves. In the UK, I didn't
have the time to do any charitable work like this. Some of
the horses I shod were worth into many thousands of
pounds and I didn't have some young person who got no
qualifications in farriery telling me how I should do my
job. As I have said, some of these animals suffered badly
with laminitis. One came to the sanctuary and we had to
decide should we put it to sleep or give it a chance. It was
decided to give it a chance. I was certain it needed a
resection, which is where a hole is made in the outer wall
of its hoof to let out all the gunge. Bit like a blood blister
under a human's nail. Once it is lanced a lot of the pain
goes away although a bit more is involved. I had often
mentioned that other donkeys might benefit as I had had

good results with horses I had attended to with top UK vets. The new people at the donkey sanctuary never allowed me to do resections even with Yiannis, who, in his own words, told me equine was not one of Cypriot vets specialities but he was one for learning.

When I mentioned resections, I was told by a senior staff member that they didn't want me practising on their donkeys. I never did these resections for the fun of it. Also, in the UK, I had a vet in attendance with me and often it would be a joint decision. I would have worked with Yiannis and he understood how resections worked when I explained it to him and what we needed to do. This was Cyprus and Yiannis who was now the Cypriot vet for the sanctuary was always open to new ideas.

Anyway, this donkey with laminitis came in with abscesses in both front hooves and it wouldn't clear up. I was sure this case would benefit from a resection but again I was not allowed to try and help the poor thing. The donkey's old owner often called into the sanctuary to see it and would have been heartbroken if it was put to sleep. I heard the head groom telling someone he was dreading telling the old owner that he was thinking of putting the poor thing to sleep. I said, 'Well, if you are thinking like that let me have ago at a resection. Give me a week to see if there is improvement. If it works you won't have to tell the owner what you are dreading.'

So I got to do a resection only because they were too scared to tell the old owner of the donkey's fate. I did it with Yiannis and the first thing he said when I made a hole in the hoof wall was, 'Mick, it's bleeding.'

'I know, Yiannis, and don't pull your hair out just yet, there is probably more to come.'

Everybody around at the time thought I was butchering the donkey's hooves, but a week later there was a big improvement. Six weeks later the animal was still living and walking around the paddock as happy as Larry. That is how I got Yiannis to understand how it worked and we did many others the same. That was until I was not allowed to do these resections when another UK person visited the sanctuary.

This happened after John and I did the usual Tuesday morning when we attended to the donkeys. Another newcomer had been admitted and the poor thing could hardly stand up. When it did, it stood right back on its heels rocking. I thought I didn't have to be a brain surgeon to diagnose what was wrong and felt its hot hooves, plus it had raging pulse. Yiannis had, at the time, gone down with a dose of the flu so couldn't attend. I rang him at his home and I said that I thought that a resection was needed. Straight away he said, 'Do it, I trust you.'

So with John's help, I managed to make a little resection the best we could do. It was a case of doing a little and letting the poor thing have a rest. A few days later on the Friday morning visit, we could see a small improvement and at least the donkey could stand. Yiannis had recovered enough to be able to attend and I asked him if he would sedate as there was more pus and gunge still to be let out. A few months later, this animal was walking around the paddock with not a care in the world. I thought the person who had flown out from the UK was going to say, *Mick, you worked wonders on this donkey*, but she didn't. When she saw the holes made from the resection which had started to grow out, she said, 'This donkey needs to be put to sleep. The holes in the hooves will never heal.'

I tried to reassure her that they would eventually grow out like all the others, but no, she didn't want to know. Even if they didn't, did it matter, the donkey was not in any pain and I think it would rather have holes in its hoof wall if it meant not suffering. So the poor thing was put to sleep and I began to think I was not allowed to prove her wrong and me right. After that case, I started going home moaning to my wife about the place. I even rang a top farrier, Doug Bradbury, who was at the time a senior person on the UK farriers' examination board and a top vet, John Coupe. I had started to doubt myself and wanted to ask them if I had done anything wrong. Both assured me they would have done the same. They both wrote a reference for me, saying I was an experienced farrier who they both had known and had worked with me for many years and would trust me with any equine animal. When I tried to show these letters to the sanctuary, they didn't want to know. I thought of the many clients who had expensive horses that I had to shoe in the UK and the owners trusted me enough to shoe them. Now I was starting to doubt whether I was good enough to trim a donkey's hoof.

HORSESHOEING

Julie and Kleanthis, George Hourie's friends, who we had the barbeque with, and whose horse's hooves I had once trimmed, got in touch with me. Julie asked if I could put shoes on one of her horses. She had got the shoes that were taken off months earlier as it was not being worked. So it was just a case of a refit and although I never intended to shoe horses in Cyprus I thought I needed more of a challenge now the donkey sanctuary had made me feel if I wasn't good enough. After all, trimming a donkey's hooves was not hard and even some of the foot problems that the donkeys had were just routine to me where others thought different. At the time, I felt I was expected to let my standards drop to a level that was not acceptable to me. I was still hurting over the donkey that was put down for no reason at all, just because someone didn't want to prove that I was right. I needed a lift. I knew I knew more than some of the folk that had flown out from the UK. One day I got my chance to find out how much they really did know. One of the donkeys I had got to trim had a bit of thrush in its frogs. I knew they would want to inspect it and make a big drama. So I told John and a lady who worked in the sanctuary gift shop we were going to invent a special name for thrush when this character was ready to inspect.

When it got looked at, I said, 'The correct name for thrush is pedal mortis.

'That is correct,' I was told by this know-it-all.

The lady from the shop had to walk away as she couldn't help herself as she was going to burst out laughing. She knew we had just invented a name and this person had fallen for it. I suppose with not knowing as much as they thought, they wanted to impress me by showing they knew all the proper medical terms. Unfortunately for that person, "pedal mortis" is not a technical term for thrush. More than likely, if it had pedal mortis, rigor mortis would be involved and the poor thing would have been dead.

So I went and shod Julie's horse. I think it was her who told a riding school, who then told a bigger one, and in no time at all my, name had gone all round Cyprus. I had found a business in Nicosia that stocked horseshoes and tools owned by a man called Panos. I was now back working – not full-time but as busy as I wanted to be as a farrier. I say nearly as I wanted to have days where we went with friends for meals and did other social activities. We had joined the P3A, similar to the U3A in the UK. So I just tried to work two days a week. OK, sometimes three or four days. I still did the donkey sanctuary and tried not to get involved in the veterinary side. The Vettec that was used on donkeys with problem feet had been discarded. I was told to stop using it on donkeys where grit caused abscesses infecting the white line of the hoof. I had used it on one that didn't like walking on the rock-hard ground. I found putting Vettec on it lifted its sole just enough not to touch the ground. When the sanctuary decided not to use it, the animal was crippled. It didn't stop them asking me for my opinion though. I thought, why bother no one would listen anyway. I suppose I was getting past caring. If I didn't see the problem, it wouldn't bother me.

So with the horseshoeing getting more and more busy, I felt something would have to give or I would end up working seven days a week. I had gone to live in Cyprus for an easy life and often thought, did I want to carry on with the donkey sanctuary? When Mary and Patrick were in charge, I enjoyed the hustle and bustle of the life there. It felt like a family and now this family life had disappeared. Then one Friday morning, I did leave.

It happened when a lady I will call Jane asked me if I could shoe her horse before she went on holiday. Her friend was going to be looking after her horse and it needed a new set of boots. Jane didn't want to burden her mate with having to get it shod, so she asked me if I could fit her in before her holiday. By this time, I had shod Jane's horse several times and it was very flat footed and not sound when I first took it on. Now, though, she was competing and getting good results at show jumping only after two or three shoeings. As I have said before, Cypriot farriers have never taken a stiff examination like British farriers have and how this lady's horse was shod showed this. I think the way this horse was once shod looked to me like someone had thrown its shoes on from over the stable door. It was made to look more flat-footed than it really was. With me, when I took Jane's horse on, I felt I needed a horse with foot problems to give me a lift and I think Jane's horse did that for me. When Jane asked me to shoe her horse before she left for her holiday, I said, 'Friday morning, 7:30am. I will come to you first before the donkey sanctuary.'

I rang the sanctuary to tell them I would be arriving around 9am as I'd got a horse to shoe en route. I didn't see any problem, the donkeys on the list I had to attend to were not a problem and I didn't need any grooms to help me as John was with me. Well, that is what I thought. When John and I arrived at the sanctuary, the grooms were having their 9am coffee break. So when I arrived with John, we joined them for a coffee. Nothing was said to me about us arriving late. In fact, it was normal jovial banter. Once the break was over, a senior member of staff more or less told me I was contracted to the donkey sanctuary on Tuesdays and Fridays and I should put them first. Well, my reply was, 'I'm not contacted to anyone. I never had a contact in my life.' I was 62 years old at the time and I had come to Cyprus for an easier life.

At my time of life, I didn't want to be tied to contracts. If I chose not to work on a particular day for some reason, I wanted to be able to. I doubt I would have wanted to shoe horses again if I hadn't needed a lift from being put down too many times by the sanctuary. I felt I needed to prove to myself that I was a better farrier than I was made to believe, something that I had never had to do in the UK. So that Friday morning is the day I told the sanctuary to find another farrier. I suppose it had been coming as I had been moaning to Phyl about the place for several months. When I got home that day, Phyl saw I had a mischievous smile on my face and asked, 'What I have you been up to?'

'Well, the shit hit the fan this morning,' I replied, probably smiling ear to ear. 'I told them to get another farrier. I was supposed to be contracted to the donkey sanctuary on Fridays.'

I didn't leave them in the lurch, though, I gave them a month's notice to find another farrier although I did agree to still to do one or two outreaches. At least on the outreaches, lots of the Cypriot folk liked what I did and accepted any advice from me.

MOVING HOUSE

Two years after moving to Cyprus, Phyl and I moved again to a village called Koili, spelled Killie in English. Our new home had unobstructed views of the valleys below and Troodos Mountains in the distance. Our first home was in a little cul-de-sac but we felt it to be too British. We wanted to live the Cypriot way now we were living in Cyprus. Too many British folk wanted Cyprus to change to the British way of life. The only trouble with our new home was it wasn't habitable when we bought it. It needed a total refurbishment. The garden was overgrown but it had several lemon trees, a grapevine, a pomegranate tree and a fig tree. We could see through the muck and bullets and had a vision of what the potential was and we had heard through the grapevine it was for sale, but we didn't know who the seller was. Yiannis – yes, another Yiannis – who at one time was the muktha (mayor of the village) was the man to ask who knew everything about the village. To our surprise, although he knew who the owners were, he didn't know the property was for sale. So after two or three phone calls he located the two brothers who owned the place. We agreed a price and two months later we had found a British builder to do the renovation for us. What attracted us to this guy was he came from Leicestershire and one of his cousins who built new houses was an old client of mine. I knew the cousin had a good name in the building world so just assumed his relation was the same.

One night while having a meal outside Lagis's coffee shop in Koili, a local guy came to tell me I had not got the best builder. I thought this to be sour grapes because I had not asked a Cypriot builder. Two years later, what the guy had said to me about builders were still echoing in my head. Although the renovation looked fine on first glance, with a new swimming pool in the garden, we ended up having to spend thousands having shoddy workmanship put right. Doors didn't fit, the new roof that the builders put on had more holes in than our kitchen colander. The patio at the back of the house had sunk into the garden, not to mention the many water pipes that leaked inside the house. We even had to take a stud wall down to repair one leaking water pipe joint.

Talking of water pipes leaking, alarm bells sounded when we were moving from our home at Chlorakas to Koili. The builder hadn't finished working on our house but he had started work elsewhere. Although our house was now habitable, it was far from finished but we were told we had running water. When we went to give the place a good clean before moving in, we found we didn't have water when we turned the taps on. I went to investigate and found a stopcock next to the water header tank on the house roof turned off. As soon as I turned it, I heard a whoosh of water running down the pipes. The trouble was Phyl heard a whoosh of water running in the guest bathroom. When she opened the door to the bathroom, she got soaked head to toe. Water was squirting out of many pipe joints and cascading everywhere. I was on my way down from the roof when I heard Phyl scream at me to turn the water off. When I saw how wet Phyl was, I nearly burst out laughing but I thought better of it as I liked living.

I think the builder classed us as moaners because we were pestering him with water pouring down the walls and thought that was our problem. He always seemed to have an excuse for his shoddy workmanship. He wanted us to wait from the Tuesday until the weekend to fix it. He didn't class our predicament an emergency. I assured him if he wanted his last payment he had to come now.

When we finally got moved in, the plastering needed more attention and when his guys came back to fix it they managed to plaster our bed, bedside cabinets, floor mats and just about everything else in the room. What had got me hot under the collar was we had offered to move our furniture and put dust sheets down. We were told they would move things and cover anything that was too big or awkward to move. When we saw the mess, we were so annoyed as they hadn't covered anything with dust sheets. I got on the phone to the builder to complain. He then tried to say his guys had worked hard for us and not to complain. I was going to complain as they had a total disregard for our belongings. Also, he wanted us to pay the electrician separately. That was when I said I had another complaint when I found my electric drill and other electrical tools that his electrician had helped himself to from my shed and just left them out in the pouring rain. When I checked the agreement, his quote included the electrician and in future they had to bring their own equipment.

There were other payments he was trying to add on too which was not on the original quote. I was glad

I never gave into his demands as we had to have major electrical wiring done a few years later. I even tiled a wall myself as one of this guy's staff told me the reason the wall never got tiled was because the wall was too wonky. Well, they had built the wall.

We ended up getting other workmen in to put right the builder's shoddy work. Once we got everything put right, our new home was suburb. One part of the house had its own self-contained annex which we rented out to holiday makers. The swimming pool was a godsend in the long hot summers. We could always find a lemon whatever time of the year and they were not like the titchy little things in the UK we have to pay 40p each for. Pomegranates, figs and nectarines trees were loaded with fruit. In fact, we gave loads to friends rather than let it go to waste. We had more than we could ever eat.

On another topic, we could get English television if a bloody great big satellite dish was on the roof. When we first moved to Chlorakas we got away with a smaller one, but transmission frequencies got changed so we needed an even bigger one. Alan, an electrician we had got to know, had erected one for us at Chlorakas and when we moved to Koili, he took it down and erected it for us at our new home. Often, we did have trouble with satellite signal and especially on Channel 5. The signal always seemed to break up at adverts on the last part of a film at around seven o'clock in the evening when you really wanted to know what happened. I think it was Alan who told me that if a roof slate is placed on a certain place in the dish, it can restore reception. So regularly I could be seen on our roof at the commercial break with my mobile ringing Phyl's phone trying to place a slate in the exact position to regain Channel 5. Phyl would be telling me when I had hit the television G-spot. Years later, other means of transmission had come on the market as the big dishes were becoming obsolete.

Our view from our garden and more railings I built.

SUNDAY LUNCH

'You and Phyl fancy Sunday lunch at the Vatouthkia restaurant with us?' John and Gill asked.

'Sure, John, but we have Phyl's friend, Pam, staying with us.'

'That's OK, bring her along too. But first, Nikos, the owner of the restaurant, wants his donkey's hooves trimmed.'

I knew where the Vatouthia was but had never had a meal there or met Nikos. His restaurant is on the outskirts of the village of Kamares near to Paphos. It is situated down a rough track that leads eventually to Adonis baths in the middle of nowhere. It is advisable to book as Sunday lunches are very popular.

John and Gill had gone there for a meal a few days before and had spotted a donkey that was in the need of a foot trim on land next to the eatery. They happened to mention to Nikos that they were friends with me, and I was a farrier and were sure I would attend to his donkey. John arranged to meet me with Gill at our house and while John and I went off to do this donkey's hooves, Gill went for a swim in our pool. I had never met Nikos but knew his father who was the postman in our village. John and Gill had told me beforehand not to charge him as we got to go and have Sunday lunch and it would be on the house.

We had been led to believe the old donkey could be awkward but we found it to be the opposite. When we arrived to trim the donkey's feet, it just walked up to us and let John put a head collar on. I got the feeling it enjoyed any human attention and it didn't mind having its feet manicured. Nikos was busy in the restaurant kitchen preparing Sunday lunch for a fully booked sitting and I could understand he didn't have time to get involved. In no time at all we were finished and when we were leaving, he gave us a wave and a thumbs up sign, knowing he would see us later.

Sunday lunch at the Vatouthia is well worth a visit. The salad bar must be a 20-foot-long table with such a huge variety that I thought my plate might not be big enough if I wanted I bit of everything. That is just for starters. Then a very generous portion of either pork, beef, or both, plus chicken and vegetables and to finish off a variety of deserts. Then all diners got asked if they would like a brandy or a liqueur on the house.

At the time, the price to trim the donkey was 20 euros. Nikos's Sunday lunches at the time were 12 euros each plus drinks and five of us ate and drank for the equivalent of four euros. Nikos wouldn't even accept any money from us for the drinks. I suppose trimming the donkey was nothing to me, and the food was nothing to Nikos. So roughly every two months we ate at the Vatouthia with John and Gill for next to nothing. On another occasion, we had our friends, Steve and Bev, staying and Nikos insisted we bring them along too. We did go on many other occasions and paid when not on donkey duty though.

One day, Nikos asked me to have a look at a swelling on his donkey's navel. It looked as like something had stung it although I couldn't see any puncture wounds. The donkey didn't look to be bothered by whatever caused the swelling and I was sure it would go down. Two days later, on a Thursday morning, I went back to see the donkey and sure enough the swelling had subsided, to Nikos's relief.

I found with Cypriots once you make friends with them, they appreciate anything that you do for them and Nikos liked to show his appreciation. That Thursday morning, he had a couple of beers waiting when I had looked at his donkey. He just wanted to have a chat with me. Nothing in particular, just like two old mates when they meet up for a natter. I suppose we talked for an hour or so and two pints later I was getting ready to leave. Nikos, though, wasn't satisfied he had only given me two beers on the house but gave me a big bag of apples too. Then he invited Phyl and me to the entertainment that his restaurant put on every Friday night. It was a group of young people dancing to music played by two musicians. He had saved a table for us near to the dancers. I was not sure if it was my sort of entertainment, but I was wrong. The group of young people who performed were brilliant. We didn't want the show to finish. Nikos again had a wonderful spread of food that was so tasty. More a barbeque and salad bar on Friday nights, plus our table seemed to get a never-ending supply of drink. When it was time for home I went to pay and Nikos wouldn't let me. He appreciated what I had done for him.

We had many a good night at Nikos's and it wasn't just for a meal. He started putting on other music shows. Again, some of the acts had flown in from the UK. I remember one guy in particular who was a Phil Collins tribute act. He was so good if you closed your eyes, you would have thought it was Phil Collins himself singing. Then he had an Abba tribute who again were superb and the many other acts too. It felt like years ago in the UK when a nightclub was to have a nice meal and watch a show afterwards. Not like today where music is blasted so loud in a thud-thud beat and nothing much else happens because you can't talk or hear anybody for the noise. As for dancing, folk are routed to the spot dangling their arms up and down as if their feet are glued to the floor (my opinion).

I still have very fond memories of the meals and entertainment at Nikos's. Life felt so good and with the endless days of sunshine; there was no better feeling than sitting having a lovely meal outdoors on warm evenings under a cloudless sky.

ANOTHER OUTREACH

It would be after I had finished doing the sanctuary donkeys but still did the occasional outreach for them. I can remember a day that really sticks in my mind. I arrived with John at the sanctuary at 7:30 one morning. We both knew it was going to be a busy day as some calls were a good hour's drive away. I can't quite remember how many donkeys we got to attend to, but it was over 20 and scattered at calls around the Nicosia and Famagusta area. Usually it would be just the four of us who would go: myself, John, Yainnis and Gill in the sanctuary's double cab pickup. That day, though, two other folk who had flown in from the UK wanted to come with us. So, in other words, there was not enough room in the pickup for John and me. We would need to go in my van. Well, at the time, I had only agreed to trim the donkeys for a set price for each animal and the donkey sanctuary would supply the transport. When I found I was expected to use my own van and clock up no end of miles, they had to agree to pay for mileage or I wouldn't have gone. To me, I was still giving my services cheap, and I wouldn't have gone if I hadn't got paid for using my own motor. How I looked at it was these other folk were just coming for the ride and, if anything, it was them that should have used their own hire car.

Anyway, on arriving at the first call around 9am, we had loads of donkeys to see to. Some were straightforward trims and a few had other problems. By the time I had finished trimming and Yainnis finished doing his veterinary work, it was getting on for midday. I smelt the aromas of food cooking. Yes, the lovely folk at this call had prepared a meze for us. There was so much food I think if another four or five more folk had turned up it wouldn't have mattered. The meze was so tasty we couldn't help having more than we should have done. Yes, these folk seemed happy what we did for them and paid very generously for our services. The only trouble was they were too kind.

On arriving at the next call, my stomach felt it was bursting as it was filled to capacity. It felt I needed to lay down and rest after such a big meal rather than trim donkey's feet. I knew I was overdoing it when I ate the meze. It was as if one side of my brain was saying, *I shouldn't be stuffing myself*, but the half was saying, *what the hell*. After forcing myself to bend, I did manage to attend to the other donkeys at the many calls we got that afternoon.

The other thing that got me with a lot of Cypriots was they never gave their animals a name. If it was a donkey that's what it got called, a donkey. A dog would be dog and so forth. So when Gill wanted to log what was done to each donkey we often had to think of a name for future reference. This particular day – I am not sure if it was the last call or not – Gill asked the owner what the names of their two donkeys were. Again, it was what we had heard so many times before. We were told, 'No names.' So again we had got to think of something to log theses donkeys by. John had happened to look at his watch and it was five o'clock and that is what one got named Five o'clock, and the next one became Half-past five.

On another outreach on another day, and this time it was just Gill, John and I, we had a call where there were donkeys and two ponies. The donkeys gave us no problem but the ponies were not the normal size but miniature. Years ago, I once had some Falabella horses on my books but even they looked large compared to these two ponies. Even getting down on my hands and knees to trim their hooves proved difficult. I felt I needed a nail file instead of a rasp and I certainly didn't need clippers. A few good rubs with the rasp was all I needed to do but getting to do it was another thing. That was when John had the bright idea and got his hands under the pony's belly and lifted them to chest height. So that is how we went about trimming these miniature ponies on odd occasions we had to attend to them.

Yes, these outreaches were interesting I met some wonderful characters and I got to see places of Cyprus that lots of holiday makers wouldn't know existed. I am sure when someone holidaying went exploring the little Cypriot villages and saw old men sitting outside coffee shops, they probably thought the locals were staring back at them. Well, I often wondered that sometimes John and I were the ones staring back. We had often got invited to join the locals for a Cypriot coffee after seeing to their donkeys.

Riding schools

I had another lady get in touch with me who kept her horse in a do-it-yourself-livery stables. The place was one you can say was a bit of a ramshackle set up. Anyway, for me it didn't worry me that the stables had seen better days as long as the horses behaved themselves while I shod them. This client who I will call Gemma was ready and waiting when I arrived and her horse stood as good as gold. Gemma said her horse's hooves always looked as if they needed a good trim even after they had just been shod. I had to agree with her they did look a bit long in the toe before I started. What I did find was there was I load of dead sole that needed to be pared off. If this wasn't removed the growth of the wall of the hoof would get left and the shoes fitted over it. This often was why lots of horses looked to have long toes even when newly shod. I found this problem many times as sometimes with the hot climate and dry terrain this dead sole can be sometimes quite difficult to pare off. Often, how I saw it, the Cypriot farriers didn't try and shod the horse, leaving an excess of overgrown hoof.

The trick I had for making this dead sole easier to trim off was to either place a hot shoe on the foot as if it was to be fitted. This sometimes works to soften the sole. Failing that, I used a blowlamp and wafted the flame over the sole for 30 seconds or so. That worked every time for me.

While I was shoeing Gemma's horse, another lady asked me if I could have look at her horse as it dragged its hind feet when it was ridden. My first thought was, is it the rider. Some folk just let their horses plod along like a person does when walking with their hands in their pockets and shuffling along. I remember a stables in the UK years ago where I shod the horse's normal one year and had no problems. Then the next season, with a different batch of stable hands, lots of the same horses dragged their back feet. The following year, again with new staff, all the horses were shod normal with not a hint of them dragging their back hooves. I put that down to the riders not the horse. Not that the animal can put their hands in its pockets but if a horse is allowed to shuffle along with its head down when ridden, it is more than likely it is going to round off the toes of the hind hoof. Although this can be the likeliest cause, it can be that the horse can have some sort of a problem. My first thought was to roll the toe of the shoe to see if that helped. When I told the owner what I wanted to try, to see if it helped, she was over the moon. The lady didn't even realise that horseshoes came in various adaptions for different problems. Her previous farriers didn't do anything like that. All they fitted were bog-standard readymade horseshoes. After all, I suppose that was all they could do. None had a forge to make adjustments. All the horses had to have bog-standard ready-made horseshoes, fitted cold, and by the look of many, they didn't fit very well either.

So I ended up shoeing this other horse. I did wonder if I done the right thing as the owner, I felt, could be a bit difficult if things didn't turn out right for her. Six or seven weeks later she rang me, over the moon. Her horse's shoes were still in good fettle but it would need shoeing in a week's time. They had never lasted that long before and putting a roll on the toe certainly helped. The only trouble was at my first appointment at this yard, I went to shoe one horse, I ended up doing two. Then four more owners asked me if I would shoe theirs, so the next time I had six to shoe.

Paphos of the Third Age

I had also got asked by the Paphos Third Age (P3A), like the U3A in the UK, if I could give a short talk about farriery. Caroline Penman had very kindly offered the use of one of her horses and stables for my lecture to take place. At the time I wasn't Caroline's farrier, but I knew of her. I didn't have to shoe the horse but explained to the P3A members what the job entailed. Unfortunately, on this horse, the balance was all wrong. In fact, how it was shod made the horse look as if it was flat-footed. The horse's toes were left far too long and to me it looked as if the heels were dressed far too low. In other words, it would be like a human wearing shoes with the heel fitted on the toe of the shoe and flat were the heel is supposed to be.

I didn't know at the time if Caroline was a big friend of her farrier, so I had to grovel my way, trying my best not to offend. Luckily many of my audience didn't have a clue what I was saying and to most of them it was over their heads anyway. Some did say they found the talk fascinating and never realised so much was involved in fitting horseshoes. Some thought that a horse's hoof was like a solid mass of bone-like structure attached to the end of the horse's leg. They didn't know inside the hoof is the strongest and lightest bone called the pedal bone (it's got to be light so the horse can pick its feet up, and strong because it's got to take the whole weight of the horse). Not to mention blood vessels and nerves and why it doesn't hurt the horse when the shoe is nailed on. Also, if a horse is to perform well, it needs good balanced hooves and this one's feet were far from balanced.

Anyway, I think I managed to explain the basics of what a farrier's job is. I got the feeling that many of the audience still had no idea if this horse was shod good or bad, but I still got asked questions like, 'Does the hot shoe hurt the horse?' Some were surprised to learn that a horse needed to be shod every six weeks as they didn't know horses' hooves grow like our finger nails. None asked me about the more technical aspects of horseshoeing. I think if this group of folk had ever owned a horse, or were horsey, I may well have had to answer more in-depth questions.

A few weeks later, Caroline asked me if I could help her out as her farrier, George (another George, not George Hourie, my friend) had a back problem. Caroline at the time did rides for holiday folk who wanted to explore Cyprus on horseback. Her stables were in an amazing part of Cyprus with forests and tracks ideal for horse riders. One of her horses, according to George, was not the best behaved. Well, this was the horse that had stood perfectly for me when I did my talk to the P3A. I don't know what he classed as badly behaved but this horse stood perfect for me to shoe too. As for the flat feet, once I had shortened its toes by a mile and did minimum dressing of the heels, it looked a normal horse foot.

Another time, Caroline asked if I could shoe one of her young horse's hind feet. George thought it may be too difficult without sedation. By this time, I had got to know George and found that at other stables he was quite handy to sedate any horse himself if he thought it may misbehave without giving it the benefit of the doubt first. Most of those I did that he had said were dangerous, I never found that bad. Anyway, this young horse of Caroline's I was expecting to have a little struggle with, but didn't think it would be bad enough to be sedated. In no time at all I had got hind shoes on. There was no struggling and I thought if all youngsters stood this well when first shod I would be more than happy. I was 64 years old at the time and I think told Caroline to say to George, 'Look, Mick is over 30 years older than you and he shod the youngster, what's the problem? You can't have an old guy upstaging you.'

Over the years I shod many times for Caroline. I got the feeling if any of her horses developed a problem, she got me to see to it. I enjoyed fixing any hoof problems.

I did meet George at Episkopi riding stables. I had heard that one horse there was a nightmare for him to shoe and he would always sedate it himself. I found he was a bit too quick to get his syringe out on many horses which I would have classed as no problem. In the UK, a qualified vet has to administer any type of drugs but in Cyprus those rules didn't seem to apply. Episkopi riding school had heard about me and got in touch with me to shoe some horses for them which included this "wild one". I think they were just sounding me out as the ones I shod just stood still while I shod them.

Whilst I was there, George turned up. They hadn't booked him and I think somebody had told him I had been asked to shoe two or three horses. He introduced himself to me and watched me shoe the first horse before he left. I thought he was going to accuse me of pinching his work, but he seemed friendly to me. A month or so later he got in touch asking me how I would go about shoeing a Shire horse. The trouble with George, I found out later, was he would never admit he didn't know and this time he was blaming dodgy steel he had used to try to make the shoes for this Shire. He had attempted to shoe it by making his own horseshoes as he couldn't buy readymade horseshoes big enough. After all, there were only a hand full of Shire horses in Cyprus and most were not shod. So I could understand the farrier supplier not stocking horseshoes that big.

He said the horse was forever losing its shoes and the owner insisted that the steel he used for the shoes was too light. He asked me to meet up with him and was still blaming the dodgy bar of steel rather than himself. I don't think he had ever seen a Shire horse before and when he showed me the shoes he made, I could see why. Although he used a flat bar of steel to make the Shire's shoes, it was not heavy enough. It would have been fine on a 12.2 pony but not on this giant horse's feet. Also, when he got them made it looked to me they had been chopped down in size to try to make them fit. The size of the steel he had used would have looked a bit like the Shire horse having racing plates on its hooves. I think the reason it was always losing its shoe was it was just twisting them off. I had an idea I would have to make my own shoes when I got there, and I had put a bar of 1.1/4 x 1/2 in my van I had left over from building my fence at home.

I set to work making these large, heavy horseshoes in the gas forge out of the back of my van on a summer's afternoon with the temperature in the high 30s. When folk moan about having to work when the temperatures reach the high 20s in the UK, they don't know what blazing hot temperatures are.

George would trim and prepare the front feet while I set about making the shoes. I was thankful considering how hot it was at the time that the owner only wanted front shoes fitted. Before I cut the steel to the size I needed, I wanted to check for myself as George had said I would need 22 inches in length. Well, I know Shire horses can have big feet but this one was nowhere that big. He watched me measure across the widest part of the foot, double it, and add two inches. Normally if the horse was of normal size, I would do the same and only add one inch. This one measured eight inches across so by my calculations I would need 18 inches. How George came to 22 inches puzzled me and I asked, 'What made you think you needed 22 inches of steel? How did you measure the foot, George?'

'I got a bit of string and measured around the outer edge of the hoof and added a bit on.' With two fingers on each hand spaced apart, he indicated roughly how much he added on. 'Would that be why they came out too big, Mick?'

I must say, making those Shire shoes, I must have lost a couple of stone in weight through sweating. Well, I like to think I did because my shirt was stuck to me. Sweat poured off me by the bucketful. In the UK, when the Leicestershire branch held a horseshoeing competition, I used to joke with the lads competing that if they sweat they would be disqualified. One can't help to perspire next to a forge, even on a cold day. Imagine when the air temperature is in the high 30s and then opening the gas forge door – the blast feels like 1000 times hotter than the sun on a hot summer's day.

I finally got the shoes made and fitted without having to chop them down to size. The horse owner looked pleased with my work and praised me for how professional it looked, then turned to George and said, 'I am not paying you today, George.'

I thought, *what, he is not going to pay?* I was just about to say something I could have regretted later when horse owner continued, 'No, I am not paying you today, George. I am going to pay Mick instead.'

I thought, *thank God for that.* If he had waited another second before he said he was paying me, I might have talked back to him with words that are not in the Queen's English.

NORTHERN CYPRUS

As the months passed, I had more folk from the length and breadth of Cyprus asking for my services. Now when I look back to my life as a farrier in Cyprus, I can't believe how in such a short space of time, so many horsey folk got in touch with me. I had never advertised my work or had my name on the side of my van. It was the same when I shod horses in the UK; I didn't have my van sign written. All my work was through word of mouth. New clients, when they got hold of me, would often say I had been recommended to them by someone who I had as a client. Recommendations and word of mouth are the best forms of advertisement. All my working life I have never asked anyone to shoe their horses. I want the client to ask me, rather than me to offer my services.

What did surprise me was my farrier work got known over the border in the Turkish area too. I got a call from a lady called Di who lived in the Turkish side of Cyprus. Di had a small riding school, plus two of her horses were broken into harness. The carriage which they pulled was for weddings and also she did riding holidays for folk who wanted to explore the island on horseback. Di had got in touch with me as the farrier she used, who I will call Lagis (not his real name), again from the south side, was unreliable and had a drink problem.

I had met this guy a year or so before when I was with John when attending to a donkey outreach for the sanctuary. All we knew about that donkey was it could be a swine for Lagis when he trimmed its hooves. When we arrived at the call, we saw the donkey in a paddock and the lady in charge said she would be with us in a moment as Lagis had arrived to shoe the horses. John shouted to the donkey and it came trotting over as if it was pleased to see us. John attached a lead rope to the head collar it was wearing. I picked a front foot up and must have trimmed a good couple of inches off an overgrown hoof. We were both expecting it to be a handful as that was what we had got told. I thought maybe it is on the hinds it can be difficult.

By the time the lady who was attending to Lagis got back to us, we had finished. She was amazed that the donkey didn't give us any hassle as it could be an absolute sod not only to trim but to catch too. That would be why it was already wearing a head collar. That day was when John and I got introduced to Lagis by the lady owner. She told him that the donkey never moved an inch when we trimmed its feet. Lagis made an excuse that he had got its feet not to hurt through having white line disease. All the years I have shod horses I can safely say that I am sure that donkey had nothing wrong foot-wise. As for white line disease, I am sure this one hadn't had it either. That was the day he told John and I that no one in Cyprus could touch him for his farrier skills as he was the best farrier in Cyprus because the man himself told us he was. Over time, I noticed some of the horses that were supposed to have foot problems was because of white line disease according to Lagis. In my eyes, I couldn't see anything too much wrong apart from they had been shod in a slapdash manner.

Getting back to Di, she had many issues regarding the welfare of her horses' hooves and again it was nothing to do with Iagis's work. One in particular was a grey that looked as if it had shoes on more suited to Alibaba. This horse did have very flat feet but it looked worse because of how it was shod, and it was not exactly lame but not sound either. Also, when I saw it, it had lost one shoe after only being shod for a couple of days, and that was six weeks before. So for five weeks, that horse struggled to walk over any rough hard ground without its shoe. When I took Di's work on, I never had one bit of trouble with that horse and I got a bit big-headed when folk told me it didn't look so flat-footed.

Anyway, after Di had pleaded with me to shoe her horses even though it was a two-hour journey for me, I did enjoy the challenge. She offered to pay me a very generous travelling allowance. She paid for the yearly insurance for my van that the Turkish authorities insisted we had to pay even though the motor was insured in the south. Then she paid my charges for shoeing her horses and never once asked me for a "special price".

I had only been over the border once before and had taken out insurance for the day which looked straightforward so I thought, no problem. That first day I went to shoe Di's horses, she would meet me at the border. She would pay for the year's van insurance at the same time and she thought it was easier for me to follow her to her stables rather than give directions. The trouble that day was there was no one to issue the insurance and without it I wouldn't be allowed to enter the Turkish territory. I was glad Di had come to meet me as she could speak a bit of Turkish and she looked to me to be a lady who didn't take any nonsense. The official at the passport office looked as if his life was in danger with how Di was speaking to him about how we were unable to buy the required insurance. He was soon on the phone to the insurance man from whatever she said to him. I thought if it was anybody else, he wouldn't have cared and that would be their problem. I think the way Di spoke and looked at him, he thought he had better react if he wanted to live another day. He seemed to know who to talk to and we were informed somebody was en route to issue me with the document I needed.

The trouble is in the Greek side of Cyprus, these official folk never seem to rush themselves. The Greek Cypriots have a saying, "siga siga", that's sounds like "cigar cigar" and it doesn't mean that you smoke a couple of cigars while you wait. No, that would mean it to be quicker. Siga siga means slowly slowly, and that may mean things get done that day if you are lucky. So when I heard someone was en route to deal with us, I hoped they weren't going to call to see this client and that client before they got to me. I just hoped the Turkish system wasn't like it was on the Greek side and that it meant now rather than tomorrow.

We didn't have to wait that long. Well, two cups of coffee long before a guy turned up to issue me with an insurance certificate and we were on the way. At the time I thought she must have really trusted me to be paying a year's insurance when she had not seen my work. She had only heard about me from some of her horsey pal in the South.

Di's stables were in a village just on the outskirts of Kyrenia. The yard was all concrete, spotlessly clean and a perfect set-up for shoeing horses. She employed two grooms, Adee (I think that is how he spelt his name) who was Turkish, and a guy from Bulgaria. Both guys were very helpful and were on hand if I needed help.

I know the climate in Cyprus is hot and you need to quench your thirst quite regularly, but not beer while shoeing horses. I have said Lagis had a drink problem but I didn't realise how bad. Di's grooms told me Lagis drank a couple of small cans of beer to every horse he shod. That meant after shoeing Di's six horses, he could have downed 12 beers. When I saw his work, I thought the drink may have had a lot to do with the state the horses' hooves were in. None of the six horses' and ponies' shoes were fitted very well. All had shoes missing and it wasn't because Di had left it to the last minute to book him. Judging by the job, it was a case that if it was somewhat near, nail the shoe on regardless. Hind shoes for the off hind were nailed on the near hind and vice versa. As for foot balance, I don't think he knew it existed in horse shoeing. He had shod a horse which was very flat-footed and left the toes long and massacred its heels and hadn't really got a clue why it was still footy after he shod it. So to try to cover his back, he would often diagnose white line disease. I am sure Di thought differently, but with me knowing the guy it wouldn't be his work that was causing the problem because, as I have said, he had already told me he was the best farrier in Cyprus.

After one visit to Di's, other horsey folk in Northern Cyprus started to ask me about shoeing their horses.

With that happening and in summer with temperatures into the 40s, I started to do two journeys two weeks apart. John, who held the donkeys for me at the sanctuary, had started to come with me. I used to pick him up at 4:30am in the morning and we would be at Di's by 6:30 and Andee always made us a cup of tea on our arrival.

John had developed a big interest in farriery and he could tell the difference between a good and bad farrier's work. He didn't come just for a ride out, he liked to get involved in any way he could. He was very good at holding a horse that was a youngster or one that could have a bit of a frisky nature. He would talk to them and give reassuring pats. He would be stood next to the horse not four or five feet away on the end of a long lead rope attached to the horse head collar. I have often said if a horse wants to be difficult to shoe, the person holding the horse's head collar has to know what they are doing to help the farrier. I have in the past had owners who would want to hold their horse while reading a book. On another occasion, a woman thought she would help me to shoe a very difficult pony whilst holding a three-month-old baby in her arms. Reading a book and holding onto the very end of a rope attached to the horse's head collar, which is four- or five-feet-long is not holding the horse or helping the farrier. The time when a woman had her baby in her arms, I wouldn't allow it. Her pony was not at all easy and didn't she give a thought for her child? I had visions of it rearing which it did and striking the infant. That is not holding the horse. The book reader or a person who is frightened of getting hurt might as well not be there. In fact, these sort of folk can get the farrier hurt through not concentrating. With John though, I always felt comfortable when he was in charge of the handling of any horse, pony or donkey.

The other thing I found travelling up north was not to hit the rush hour traffic between 7:30 and 9am on a roundabout at Nicosia on the Turkish side. Nobody wants to be patient. The road leading to the roundabout had three lanes but one would have thought it was five lanes. Cars came over the grass verges, horns were blaring and probably from the cars that were causing the traffic jam. Sometimes it was better to close your eyes and hope for the best.

Another thing I found was that on odd occasions, the guards on duty at the border would want to check what was in the van. Most would not be too bothered and let me go on my way, but I did have a bit of a do with one or two guys. On one occasion a guard saw the stack of old worn-out horseshoes at the back of the van and pointing to the heap, shouted to me, 'YOU PAY TAX,' in slow and loud broken English.

'ME PAY TAX WHAT FOR?' I said slowly and loud in English like you do when somebody speaks odd words of the English language. Brits were brilliant at it, as if shouting loud and speaking slowly and sounding like a Doctor Who Dalek made people who didn't speak English understand you better.

He kept repeating, 'PAY TAX.'

I kept replying, 'ME NO PAY TAX,' trying to sound like they do when translating into English and trying my best to pretend not to understand and him trying not to understand me either when we understood each other perfectly. Luckily, I hadn't emptied the old worn-out shoes out of the van for a day or two so there was heaps of scrap horseshoes and he never noticed the new ones behind the gas forge. He kept insisting I had to pay tax on this heap of scrap.

Then he came up with a solution and went into his wooden cabin office and came out with two empty buckets and said, 'LEAVE HERE,' meaning if I wasn't going to fork out for the duty on a stack of old horseshoes, I had to leave them with him and collect them on my return.

'OK,' I replied and was relieved he never looked any further into the van as there were loads of new shoes, nails and God knows what else. Also, my memory that day was not good and I forgot to pick them up when I returned as requested. As far as I know, two buckets of worn-out horseshoes are still sitting in that chap's office years later.

On another occasion, another guard tried to insist I wasn't allowed to take my tools into the north. He soon changed his mind when I rang Di and told her I had got a problem. She told me to put this chap on the phone and I think he thought he would be awkward with her too. Well, he changed his mind pretty quickly with whatever Di said to him. All I heard from him was, 'Er grunt err err cough gulp OK.' He looked like his life was in danger, like the guy who had to ring the insurance man on my first trip. He turned to me and in broken English said, 'OK YOU GO,' as he hurriedly handed my phone back to me as if he was in a hurry to get rid of us. I had a feeling he didn't want to upset Di either.

DONKEY TRIM AT
A GRAPE VINE

One morning I got a phone call off a guy who wanted me to trim his donkey's hooves. His voice didn't sound to me as if he was a Cypriot but he tried to speak in broken English. With lots of other nationalities in Cyprus, I couldn't make out what part of the world this chap came from. The call went something like this, with both of us sounding like a Doctor Who Dalek.

'YOU DONKEY HOOF TRIM?' he asked in a slow loud voice.

'YES I TRIM DONKEY HOOVES,' I shout back loud and slowly.

'COME NOW YOU CAN TO GRAPE VINE I OWN.' Just like the way words that are translated from Greek to English.

'ME NO COME NOW. I COME MORNING TOMORROW.' Now I was starting to speak in broken English.

'YOU TOMORROW COME. NINE O'CLOCK.'

'I COME TOMRROW NINE O'CLOCK.'

This conversation must have gone on for ten more minutes and when I asked where his grape vine was, it took me by surprise. It turned out to be in the middle of Coral Bay. I thought it a bit strange. A grape vine in the middle of a complex of very modern villas that is slap-bang in the middle of a tourist area. Anyway, nothing surprised me as over the years I had shod horses where horses were never expected to live, and I never gave this guy's donkey another thought until the I got there the next morning.

At 9am, I arrived at the address that he had given to me and I was expecting to see a big grape vine plantation that I didn't know about. The address was easy to find but all I could see were big posh villas all with swimming pools. My first thought was the guy who owned the donkey had told me where he lived and he would show me the way to his grape vine he owned where he kept his donkey. The moment I stepped out of my motor, I saw an arm beckoning me from an open front door. The guy didn't show his face just a waving arm. I thought perhaps I had misunderstood him and he was still going to show me the way to his grape vine.

Walking to the front door, I could hear laughter from what sounded like several people. Still with no one in sight and near the open front door, an arm again waves to me as if inviting me into this person's home. Once my foot was about to set foot in the door I hear, 'Hi, Mick. How are you?' in perfect English and I see four people rolling around in fits of laughter.

I think I called them a word that begins with "b" and couldn't help laughing too. What a nice surprise I got. It was Andy Brown, my old farrier mate from Leicestershire on holiday with Emma, his other half, and Jo, an old client from years gone by and her then-partner.

So instead of trimming a donkey's hooves, we spent a morning having some beverages that were little stronger than coffee and tea next to the swimming pool. Before

I left, probably in no fit state to trim donkeys' hooves, we had arranged to meet up a few days later and go for a meal. The only day I could arrange, due to having relations staying at the time, was on the last day of their holiday.

The two couples had travelled on different flights to Cyprus and both had an evening flight back to the UK. Jo and her other half had to be at the airport check in for around 8pm whereas Andy and Emma hadn't to be at the airport until over two hours later. We had arranged to have a meal with them late in the late afternoon at Charles and Barbara's restaurant. Unfortunately, Phyl had been asked to help in the restaurant and it was just the five of us, although Phyl was there serving us our meal. We knew we would have time for a relaxing meal and Jo wouldn't be rushed to get to the airport, which was a 20-minute drive away. Andy and Emma were going to leave with them and were going to have to hang about for an extra couple of hours before their flight gate opened. With one hire car between them, I offered to drop Andy and Emma off later.

Our meal at Barbara and Charles's was superb with very generous portions with lots of wine to wash it down. I got the impression none of them wanted to go home. I noticed Jo had left it to the last minute to leave and by now the restaurant was filling up. With knowing the staff we were asked if we minded moving to the bar as the table was in demand after we had finished eating. So off Jo and her other half go to the airport and another bottle of wine got ordered and I joined Andy and Emma at the bar.

A couple of hours later it was 10 o'clock and anybody would have thought Emma had become part of the restaurant staff. If new customers were entering, she presented them with menus and wine lists. Andy seemed to be enjoying himself and catching his flight didn't seem important to him. I kept saying, 'Andy, we should be on the way to the airport, we should be there now.'

'I know,' he said as he poured himself another glass of wine.

Emma seemed to agree with him as she too poured herself another large glassful too. In the end I said, 'Look, Andy, we don't mind putting you up but you may find yourself helping me trim donkeys' feet in the morning.' I don't know if it was the thought of trimming donkeys' hooves or what but he decided they may have left it a bit fine as he finished his drink before we made a mad dash to the airport. Yes, they did catch their flight and if the truth was known, I had had a brilliant night with smashing friends and I didn't want the night to end. Even if they did miss their flight, we would have been only too happy to put them up.

George's Ranch

George's Ranch, a riding school and livery yard, which is situated on the outskirts of Coral Bay, had used the same Cypriot farrier for a good many years. The owner of the stables was a faithful client to him at the time so no reason to change. I was happy with the arrangement and only shod the odd horse that belonged to a livery or if there was an emergency. After all, their farrier did live at Nicosia which is an hour and a half drive away and I think he was grateful for me to knock on the odd lost shoe. At the time, I could see that the farrier wouldn't want to travel all that way for one lost shoe. It was the same in the UK – if a horse had cast a shoe and another farrier was at the stables, we would all tap a cast shoe back on. It not only helped the horse owner out but saved their farrier time not having to make a special trip.

I never asked or advertised my services in my life but if an owner asked me if I could shoe their horse or horses, then it was up to me to decide. I never went into a yard and praised my work or said if I thought another farrier's work wasn't up to scratch, even if I thought I could do better. Although I did have my opinion and to be fair, probably at times another farrier may have had a better idea than me. I wanted the horse owners to decide and a year or so later this had started to happen at George's Ranch. First it was now and then for the odd lost shoe. Then I would get a phone call from another owner asking, 'Mick, I don't suppose you could shoe my horse for us? It does this and that and it's not improving. Got any ideas what could be wrong?' I had had hints off some of the owners that they were not impressed with the Cypriot farrier's work, but I never said it was good or bad, even if I thought it was. I shod the horses or ponies the way I had done all my working life and wanted my work to be my advertisement.

I remember one pony in particular and the owner was told it had the dreaded white line disease and that was why the pony lost so many shoes and why the hoof walls were cracking up. Again the dreaded white line disease, but not from Lagis this time. Well, I don't know if my eyesight had deteriorated but I couldn't see any sign of white line disease. What I did see was the pony had got blooming long toes and the heels of the shoe were embedded in the foot. Or had the owner left it too long before booking the farrier? So I asked, 'When was the last time this pony saw the farrier? It looks as if it has not got shod for months.'

'Two weeks ago,' the owner replied.

'Two weeks? I thought you were going to say the appointment was overdue.'

I think I cured this "white line disease" by giving the hooves a blooming good trim and I had a stroke of luck – the pony stopped losing shoes. Also two shoeings later, there was no sign of cracks and splits in the animal's feet.

Another day, one of the grooms asked, 'Mick, can you shoe an un-shoeable pony? Will you have a go? We only want it shod in front.'

'Why is it un-shoeable? What does it do?' I asked thinking I had got some dangerous animal that could injure us all.

'It won't let you put its leg between your legs. It just rears,' came the answer.

'Well, have you tried not putting its leg between yours and working from the side?' I asked.

The pony was brought into an empty stable and, sure enough, it did rear when I tried the normal way that a horse or pony is shod. So working from the side I managed to dress the front hooves and without too much bother I got the front shoes fitted and nailed on. I thought, *well that was easy*. Over the years, I had shod horses a lot worse than this pony where the owners wouldn't have admitted their nag was plain awkward.

A year or so later I seemed to be shoeing more and more horses that were in livery at George's Ranch and one morning while clenching up and finishing the last horse, I heard my name mentioned. On looking up, I saw a face peering over the stable door and a voice saying, 'I didn't know you travelled as far as Cyprus, Mick, on your farrier round.'

'Well, what a surprise it is to see you, Pat Brown. What are you doing here?' I replied.

'I live here and am I glad to see you, come and see Mac's hooves,' she muttered.

I mentioned Pat in my first book, *All Clenched up and Nearly Finished*. She was the lady who invited me to keep our old horse, Sancho, with hers in her father's paddock at Seagrave in Leicestershire back in the early 1980s. Years later she had left Leicestershire with her husband and family and moved to the Isle of Man. She didn't know that Phyl and I had planned to live in

Cyprus but then again, I never expected her to either. Mac was a young horse she had had shipped over from the UK. At the time, he was unshod but when I inspected his hooves, I said, 'He looks to me that he needs a blooming good foot trim. When did you have him done last?'

'Last week and yes, I know what you are thinking and I am relieved you are shoeing horses in Cyprus. Can you give him a trim while you are here?' replied Pat.

So now I got the idea my old clients from Leicestershire were following me to Cyprus and wondered who else I was going to bump into.

Weeks later I was back at George's Ranch, shoeing one of the liveries when one of the grooms asked me, 'Can you shoe one of the riding school horses while you are here, Mick? It's desperate.' Bearing in mind I had never seen or met the lady who owned the stables before and I was not sure what she thought of me.

The horse I was asked to shoe had lost three of its shoes and again I asked, 'Why do you leave it to the last minute to book the farrier?'

'We didn't. He was supposed to come three weeks ago, and never turned up. A week later he assured us he was on the way and even asked if we needed anything from the shop just down the road from us as he was just calling in. That was 10 o'clock in the morning and by 5pm he still hadn't shown up.'

I know in the UK I had clients who waited until the horses' shoes were about to drop off and expected me to drop everything, but in this case they had booked the farrier weeks ago. The problem was he repeatedly never turned up time after time and was always promising not to do it again. I didn't want to see them stuck so I shod the horse for them.

Later that afternoon my mobile rang and was taken by surprise as it was Caroline, the owner from George's Ranch. It went something like this: 'Hi, Mick, thank you for sorting us out today. I wondered if you would shoe my best competing horses and one or two that have foot problems.'

'Well yes I can but I thought—'

Before I could say another word, a very annoyed Caroline butted in. 'I have been faithful to our farrier for a long time and given him many chances to change his ways, now he has let me down too many times. I was so impressed with your work and was hoping you would be happy to take us on.'

'Well yes, I suppose I can,' I sputtered as I had got caught off guard.

'I can ask Anglos to do the riding school ponies if that is OK with you, Mick.'

'Well yes, that is fine by me,' I replied.

Anglos and his mate, another Yiannis, had become big friends to me. I had got to know these two guys as they took over at the donkey sanctuary when I quit. From what I gathered, Anglos and the donkey sanctuary didn't see eye to eye about his work contract and he left after only a few weeks. I had always got on with these two and even covered for Anglos when he went on holiday. Also I found it useful for somebody to cover for me when I was on holiday too, which he very kindly did for me.

The day I arranged to shoe Caroline's horses, I didn't know Anglos was going to be there shoeing loads of the riding school horses at the same time. Yiannis, Anglos's mate, although not a farrier, held the horses like John did with me. I had noticed Anglos was working at breakneck speed in temperatures that were in the high 30s and by lunchtime he looked absolutely shattered. When lunchtime came, they asked me if I would like to have lunch with them at a taverna that was nearby. Over lunch Anglos said to me, 'Mick, have you finished your horses as I still have five more to do. The problem is I have to catch a flight tonight for a holiday in America. I feel I need to get home and rest as I feel so tired.'

'Is that why you were working flat out in this heat? Course I can help you, I hope they don't want them shod today.'

'No, I have got the ones that were desperate shod. I will let Caroline know you will do the rest,' replied Anglos.

Caroline hadn't told him exactly how many there was to shoe until he got there and she didn't know he was going on holiday. He knew she didn't mind if they were shod over two days and he felt a weight off his shoulders that I would help him out. I know some folk wonder why he didn't carry on into the afternoon but with the fierce afternoon heat from the sun it soon saps your energy. He had already started his day off at the crack of dawn and didn't stop until 12pm.

Over the years I saw a lot of Anglos and Yiannis. Yiannis had his own stables and one or two racehorses too. One evening he called into our home at Koili when he was passing. Over a glass of wine or two, Phyl and I didn't realise he had many jobs. I can remember him saying he did work for one of the hotels that did sea water sport activities. He also helped anybody who wanted help with a young horse to be broken in. He was in demand due to his gentle nature, plus he helped Anglos.

That evening he told us his life story and we got the idea he wanted to include us into his circle of friends. He wanted to give us an invitation to attend a church service where his young son was going to be christened. Afterwards he had organised food and drinks at a nearby restaurant. We were delighted that he classed us as friends and we felt honoured to be invited to his son's christening. The christening service, although a little different to how a christening is conducted in the Church of England, was an experience. We found that many Cypriots were very passionate about their Greek Orthodox religion and we found this ceremony an enjoyable experience. At the party afterwards, Yiannis introduced us to many of his family and friends. By we time we left for home, we felt we had known these wonderful folk for years.

WEDDINGS

In the 11-plus years we lived in Cyprus we have attended three weddings, one christening and two funerals. For the first wedding we had got an invite from Luka who we often socialised with at Lagis's coffee shop. He was not related to the bride or groom or his family. At the time, we didn't even know the couple who were getting married although we did know the groom's dad, Costas. We were having a meal at Lagis's with Pam, a friend of Phyl's who was staying with us on holiday from the UK, when Luka invited us to this couple's wedding reception the next day (Saturday).

All that evening he insisted and he kept assuring us it would be OK. When we left for home, his last words were, 'See you at the wedding reception tomorrow.'

When we got home, we thought, *we can't turn up, this couple don't know us*. Then it was, *then again, Luka was insisting*. Next morning, it was the same discussion again and for most of the day. *We can't go. Then again, should we?* In the end we did and went with money in an envelope for the bride and groom. When we arrived at the venue, we were relieved to see Luka sitting close to the door and in no time he introduced us to the bride and groom. Costas, the groom's dad, who we did know, was so pleased to see us there and he also told his son who we were.

Cypriots do like to greet folk with hugs and handshakes and we got plenty from not only the newlyweds but from the other guests too. We had just spent the whole of that Saturday deciding if we should we go or not. Now we were there, we found the families were pleased we came. The friendly atmosphere soon put us at ease and I thought how we had fretted all day, discussing if we should attend. We must have said the phrases God knows how many times – *should we go, we can't go, Luka said its OK, what do you think, yes let's go*, then back to, *no we can't,* then at the last minute, *should we?*

Pam had only arrived in Cyprus from the UK the day before and although we were taking her out for a meal at Lagis's coffee shop, she never expected she was going to be invited to a wedding reception of total strangers the next day.

Once the last remaining guests had arrived, we were wined and dined on food I thought that would last me a week. It was from a buffet with many of the delicious Cypriot dishes to choose from. From the amount of food and drink to choose from, I thought it wouldn't have mattered if another 20 more folk turned up. Afterwards the music started with different dances that the Cypriot folk love to do. I must confess that we tried too but our attempt may have looked more like a comedy act than the accomplished locals. Nevertheless, we were praised for having a go.

During a break in the dancing, the bride and groom appeared on the dancefloor for guests to pin more money on them. I couldn't believe the amount of 50 Cyprus pound notes they had pinned on them (this was before the currency became the euro.) I said to Phyl, 'Should we get married again in Cyprus?'

A few years later, Yiannis, the vet, got married. This time we did have a proper invitation from the bride and groom to attend and we knew many of the other guests too. Our friends John and Gill had got an invitation too so the four of us went together to the village of Anogyra. This time we had an invite to the church service too. Unfortunately, so had the other 300-plus guests! The small Greek Orthodox church couldn't fit us all in and many of us had to wait outside. We could hear the service although we Brits didn't understand a word of it. When the newlyweds appeared from the church, the cameras flashed for photos of the happy couple. Many others who couldn't fit in the church wanted to give hugs and handshakes.

Whilst this was going on, we made our way to the centre of the village where the reception was held. All the road down the main street was shut off and replaced with hundreds of tables and chairs. Once Yiannis and his wife arrived, an orderly queue was formed with folk holding envelopes that contained money. I found there was not a set figure but the usual was around 50 euros. We took our turn and 15 minutes later we were wishing the newlyweds all the best and handing over our envelope.

Again, the food and drinks were not in short supply and sitting under the stars on a warm summer's evening to celebrate the happy couple's wedding day made it more enjoyable.

FARRIER SUPPLIES

When the first riding school had got in touch with me, I needed to find a stockist who supplied farriers with horseshoes and nails. I hadn't needed new shoes when I knocked that first pair on for Julie as she already got the horse's shoes. Now I had several riding schools who wanted my services plus several other establishments. George Hourie was still in Cyprus when Julie first asked me and he told me to try a guy called Panos, in Nicosia. So off I went to Nicosia and found Panos had two farrier supply shops there. One right next to the Nicosia horse racing track. He welcomed me and although his business didn't carry the stock I was used to in the UK, he had enough to get me started. I found tools, especially rasps and farrier knives to be very expensive. I dreaded to ask him what a new pair of diamond-tipped nippers would have cost as the last pair I bought in the UK cost what I thought to be a fortune.

Anyway, at the time I still didn't think I would be that much in demand as lots of the Cypriot folk only seemed concerned with how cheap the farrier was. I thought it didn't seem to matter what the job looked like as long as the horse stayed sound and went clip-clop down the road at breakneck speed. Then when the horse developed a problem, that's when I got asked to sort it out. When it came to paying, some, not all, would want to barter a price with me which was probably less than they had paid the guy who had caused the problem. I had set my fees at ten euros dearer than the most expensive Cypriot farrier on purpose. I didn't want them to use the excuse that I was getting work because I was undercutting them. These horse owners were not like the poor folk who owned the donkeys who lived in ramshackle houses in the hills. No, some had luxury villas with a nice stable yard.

I remember one guy, who I will call Kiriakas, who thought I was robbing him. He knew what I charged before he booked me. I had shod one of his horses at a livery stable before. The owner of the livery had asked me if I could put shoes on as the guy he used said the hooves were unshoeable. The horse's hooves, although very dry and cracked, didn't look unshoeable to me. All the years I have shod horses I have never had one where I couldn't get shoes on because of the state of their hooves. OK, I have had to put extra nail holes in the shoe, or an extra clip and other adjustments but always managed to shoe the horse. Anyway, when this guy saw his horse shod later, he thought I was the best thing since sliced bread and wanted me to shoe his other four horses at his home.

He was a guy who owned several cars, all nearly new, plus lived in a massive villa with a stable yard attached. His other four horses were not the best behaved to shoe and again, just like a guy I shod for in the UK, he thought I was his best mate and should be cheaper for him. I had never met him at the livery yard and didn't really know who he was. I had only met him when he got in touch with me to shoe his other horses on recommendation from the livery yard owner. After I had got his nags shod, that was when the bartering started. I don't do bartering for somebody who can afford many luxuries. If you end up cheap for one, they tell others and everybody wants to barter. He was not a happy bunny that I had charged him the going rate and he more or less told me I wouldn't last very long in business with those prices. I told him that would be my problem and I would deal with it when it happened.

Two months later, he got in touch again and the first thing he said was, 'Mick, when can you come and can you do them for a special price for me?' I had heard that saying "special price" too many times from other establishments. It was meant to sound a good deal but the seller would have often started above the going rate on purpose and just adjusted to the right price. I think Kiriakas thought I had done the same to him.

I thought, *yes, I can do them for a special price,* and said, 'Kiriakas, since your horses are a sod to shoe, I will charge you ten euros extra per horse, OK,' hoping it would put him off me.

He laughed as he thought I was joking and said, 'You come tomorrow,' as if I was waiting on the end of my mobile for him to call. I thought he hoped he could get me to shoe them and still want to try to knock my price down.

My reply was, 'Can't come tomorrow as I am going to the UK on holiday, not back for a fortnight.'

'OK, Mick, I will ring you when you are back,' he answered.

I had lied; I wasn't going to the UK. I was hoping he would just get another farrier to shoe his bad-tempered wild horses, but two weeks later he rang me again while I was driving down the highway and before I said anything he said, 'Hi Mick, I see you are back when can you come.'

'How did you know I was back, Kriakas?' I asked, thinking he knew I never went to the UK in the first place.

'I am right behind you.' And sure enough, in my rear-view mirror, there he is flashing his lights following me down the motorway. I was grateful he spoke first or I might have told him another lie.

I did go back and shoe his horses a second time and still he wanted to barter with me. I told him if this is the episode every time it comes to paying me, I wasn't interested in shoeing his horses. It wasn't that his horses were good to shoe. In fact, you had to watch out as not only were they good at kicking out if you let your guard down but handy with their teeth too! In the end, I stopped answering his phone calls. At my time of life, not only could I pick and choose which horses I shod, I certainly didn't want clients who didn't want to pay my fees, especially ones with wild horses.

It's not the farrier's job to train horses to stand still while getting shod although lots of folk think otherwise. All my working life I have heard people talk about their farrier's patience, which have included me, say, 'Oh, my farrier was really patient and his patience is paying off, Dobbin is getting better to shoe.' The trouble was, Dobbin would have got better quicker if the owner had spent time picking his feet up and giving light taps to get them used to the farrier. If only some horse owners could hear what farriers say to other farriers about some of their client's. They may realise that they are not their farrier's best customer. I think in the end Kiriakas had got the hint I wasn't interested in shoeing his wild horses. It wasn't as if it was just one that was difficult, but all four were a pain to do.

Race horses
that had their day

I got asked to shoe four racehorses for a guy who fed oats even when not in work. In my eyes, it was like feeding the horses "rocket fuel". I know racehorses need to be fed good grub but also need proper workouts to take the sting out of the frisky nature the horse develops from being fed rich food. Well, these horses only got a workout in a school for ten minutes at the best. When ridden, they were galloped at a flat-out speed again for ten minutes even when they were unfit. He thought the way to get them fit was to make the poor horse to go flat-out regardless of if they had just been brought back into work. Also, their diet never got changed when they were not in training for racing. The guy thought that because his horses could be difficult to shoe, groom or sometimes ride, that was the making of a good racehorse.

I can remember a day when one of his horses that gave me lots of trouble every time I shod it and did my back in. Although all his four horses were not the best behaved, this one was the one I really dreaded shoeing. What didn't help were the stables were all ramshackle and looked to have been built out of what scrap wood or rusty corrugated tin sheets he could find. The floor was a dirt floor littered with brick ends with other rubbish scattered about and needed a good clear-up before I could get started. Another thing I must stress was none of these racehorses had ever come close to winning a race.

I had decided I wasn't going to attempt to shoe the horse that did my back in again, or the others. I was on the last hind foot and had nearly finished, when it floored me. I ended up laid on my back and watching the horses hooves stamping either side of my head. I somehow avoided serious injury. I had only the last few clenches to do which usually takes a couple of minutes but took a quarter of an hour. When I went to put my tool box in my van, I felt a sharp pain in my back and found I couldn't stand up straight. I was hoping that it was not something to worry about but how I had been pulled about, I had an idea I may have trouble getting out of my van when I got home. Sure enough, I did. That one horse put me out of action for three weeks. Every time I tried to get up from a chair, I had to prise myself up holding on to whatever I was near. I made my mind up that I didn't need this sort of challenge. I had retired to Cyprus for an easier way of life. I know the guy wasn't pleased when I told him I wasn't going to risk getting hurt with his wild horses. In his eyes they were top class racehorses, and I should have felt privileged to be allowed to shoe them.

HOLIDAY RENTALS

Phyl and I decided we would advertise the guest apartment attached to our house for people who wanted to go self-catering. The annex had an unobstructed view of the valleys below and in the distance, the Troodos Mountains. If you were a bird watcher, buzzards were often seen hovering and then swooping down on their prey. Sometimes eagles could be seen. Swallows would also skim the swimming pool for a drink. The garden had sun loungers next to the pool. Also, a fig tree, four lemon trees, one pomegranate, a grapevine and a nectarine tree. If the sun got too hot, folk would move their sun beds under the fig tree for shade. It was the same when parking the car if there were trees. It was a good idea to park under them as the steering wheel would get too hot to hold and the seats unbearable to sit on.

I must say we were a bit apprehensive when our first holidaymakers arrived but the review that they gave us was first-class. Then others started booking for the following year. Some became lifelong friends who we ended up socialising with. There was Steve and Bev from Scarborough who stayed with us several times over the years. We often dined out together and once took them over the border into the Turkish side. Steve had once said they would love to go over the border but their hire car supplier wouldn't allow it.

It was written in the agreement. Although lots of folk do it and buy insurance at the border, which we all have to do, the car rental company were not interested. If you were involved in an accident they may charge you the value of the car not the damage to the car. So I would advise anyone to check first.

When Steve mentioned to me one day he would love to visit the Turkish side, I said, 'We can go in our car and show you some places of interest.'

We had had several trips on our own by then and got to know many ancient archaeological sites. One of the places we took them to was Kyrenia. It has a wonderful scenic harbour with castle which is a must-visit. After exploring Kyrenia, we had a leisurely trip up the coast road and into the Fez bar restaurant which I had got to know quite well from shoeing Di's horses. We just had a drink at the Fez before taking them to an Indian restaurant which we had found on previous visits and Steve and Bev were so impressed with their meal.

The restaurant was called Bollywood. From the outside it didn't look at all inviting. No curtains or any decoration in the front window, which looked like a bare room. Once you enter the garden at the back where the dining area was in summer, it felt you had walked into a tropical paradise. Not only that, the menu had mouth-watering dishes to choose from. Dishes hardened Indian restaurant diners like Steve and Bev had never heard of and of course were very tasty too. Phyl and I had visited this place many times and were always greeted with a warm welcome. It also amused me that the waiters seemed to remember us on every visit, even by our names.

Vivian, Mick, and daughter, Holly, who became regulars had booked with us for several years and took a liking to our bearded collie, Jack. Every visit they would bring Jack a squeaky doggy toy present and he seemed to know they were coming. I have often told folk we talk to our dogs and this one particular time we would say, 'Mick, Vivian and Holly are coming tonight.' Straight away he would run up to the gate to see if they had arrived. Every car that slowed down as it passed, he would go and check if it was them. Then one car stopped and as soon as he heard their voices, his tail would wag like a propeller blade and was accompanied by an excited bark. He seemed to know which guests we were expecting by how we told him.

Karen and Debs were another couple who he loved. He associated them with being their ball boy when they played tennis in the swimming pool using soft spongy balls. Every time a ball went astray out of the pool, Jack would retrieve it for them.

Also, Karen, who worked as a chef, would cook an evening meal and Jack would get a whiff of appetising aromas from the delicious dishes she was preparing. He was not the only one to notice either. Yes, we got a whiff too. I can remember one day she was cooking some pork chops covered with garlic and various other spices when Jack thought he ought to give them a visit. I must say they did encourage him round at any opportunity and it didn't help that they would cut the fatty ends off the pork chops for him at other times. This one occasion, he went round due to the aromas he got from Karen's chops still in the oven cooking. I think it was Debs who said to him, 'Jack, they are not ready yet. It will be another ten minutes before they are ready.'

I don't know if this was a coincidence or if he understood Debs, but he just walked out of the apartment. Dead on ten minutes later, the door which was slightly ajar suddenly burst fully open and in walked Jack. They told us the look on his face said, *well, you told me to come back in ten minutes, are the chops done?*

Another time we got the family from hell staying. They had booked for two weeks but how slow that fortnight went, it felt like two years by the time they had gone home. They had two young children and on our website we had advertised that although we didn't mind young children, we were not like a resort that catered for kids. Our apartment was more suited for adults who wanted to crash out and relax from hectic work schedules next to the pool, away from other noisy all-inclusive establishments.

We didn't have many rules but one was that no glasses or glass beer or wine bottles were allowed near the pool. The other was do not jump in the pool, curling your body to bomb as if to make big splash. Water in Cyprus at the time was very scarce due to a very long dry period with no rain in sight. We even put the pool cover over at night to stop any evaporation. We had to keep water in it the best we could.

In the first hour of this family arriving, the kids had nearly emptied the swimming pool of water by bombing. Their mother had moved a little plastic table next to the pool with a long-stemmed glass full of wine plus a bottle balanced near to the edge of the table. One of the rules I had only just told them about on their arrival half an hour before. Glasses, especially long-stemmed, can accidently get knocked over very easily. We didn't mind folk having a drink next to the pool but to use the nice plastic ones that looked like the real thing that we had provided. The reason was if the drink or glass bottle got knocked over and broken and glass got in the pool it would mean emptying all the water to find any shards of glass. Even then it wouldn't be easy to find it all. A shard of glass could easily get missed and only found when someone happens to put a bare foot on it.

I had no option but to say something and the mother said, 'Oh I thought you meant the children were banned from drinking from glass glasses.'

'No, adults too are banned too. Your glass of wine can just as easily get knocked over by accident too,' I replied looking annoyed.

I got the impression she thought I was trying my best to be awkward especially when I told her the kids hadn't to bomb into the pool too. So I reminded her it said on the website that although we didn't mind children there was nothing for kids in our little village. Her husband was even worse. He didn't like the idea we were living next door. In fact, we didn't think he liked holidaying with his family. We regularly heard him shouting at his kids and making them cry. I think we preferred their children and felt sorry for them for how they got shouted at for spoiling their parent's holiday. Well, that is what he shouted at them. I always thought when you are on holiday with young children, you go to places that are more suited for kids than yourself.

Some days this guy would go off on his own to do his own thing without his family. That often included going for a run in the morning. One morning we had seen the dad go off on his morning run when Cloe, a Cypriot lady who was a near neighbour shouted, 'Eya yia evav kafe,' which means, come for a coffee.

We had hardly got sat down and just about to start to sip our coffee when we heard the woman from the family from hell shout, 'Can you come! Jack has got my husband in a corner!'

Jack had never done this to all the other folk who had booked our apartment. In fact, he was usually overfriendly with many who loved his very friendly nature. As for this guy, though, he seemed to take a disliking to him from the first time he met him, like we had too. Sure enough, the guy's wife was right, Jack had her husband in a corner and he looked more like a Rottweiler than a Bearded Collie and he was shouting, 'If you bite I will kick you!'

Phyl and I think he may have antagonised Jack like he did with his own family. Although he hadn't bitten him we think Jack thought he would put this chap in his place. By the way, we said to Jack, 'Good boy,' with a big grin on our faces. I don't know how some dogs can suss dodgy folk out.

A couple I will call Tracy and James and their 14-year-old daughter, Penny, had booked a fortnight's holiday. At the time we never saw we had a problem until this family had arrived. On our booking site we tried to be as honest as we could but with the best will in the world what suits one, doesn't suit others.

On this occasion, when Penny caught sight of Jack, she stood behind her parents and looked terrified. Then her mum and dad told us of how Penny had a phobia of dogs. No dog had ever attacked her, but we could see in her face that she looked petrified. Her parents said that they had even tried therapy and various other treatments but nothing had worked. If the poor girl was out and saw a dog being walked towards her, no matter how big or small, she would cross the road to avoid coming face to face with it.

Near our back door we had a little courtyard that did lead through a gate into the garden and swimming pool area. This gate was never shut but now we would have to make sure it was closed. Did that happen? No, it didn't. It kept getting left open. Jack did go for a wander into the swimming pool area but thankfully kept his distance from Penny. Over a period of four or five days, we all noticed, including Penny's parents, that Jack was edging nearer and nearer to them without Penny realising. Then one day, the lass happened to touch Jack not realising he was sat beside her. Jack somehow knew she needed help and just sat next to her and let her come to him rather than him force himself on her. Mind you, Jack at the time he did look like a big fluffy teddy bear. I don't know if that helped but I like to think it was Jack who knew he had to be patient for Penny's friendship. A few days later, we all heard Penny's voice shouting Jack's name as if she had forgotten she had a problem with dogs.

By the time their holiday came to an end, it brought tears to our eyes to see Penny having a photo taken with her face pressed into Jacks face and her arms wrapped around his neck. Then hugs and kisses as if she didn't want to leave him.

How did that dog know? If he had rushed up to her like he did to greet most folk that would have done more harm than good. He just bided his time over a few days and edged closer to her without her realising. We were informed a few years later that she is now working with police dogs. All the therapies she had tried hadn't worked until she met Jack. He was the therapy she needed and thankfully that garden gate kept getting left open. We were so proud of him that he was all that young girl needed to get her over her phobia.

We used to get a visit from Harry who was a well-known local inhabitant of the village! Many folk often asked, 'Who the hell is Harry?' Well, Harry often gave us a visit but he would turn up unexpectedly. He decided to show his face when two very attractive young ladies in their early 20s were staying. One could probably understand why Harry took an attraction to these females like I am sure most males would. These young lasses would often be seen sunbathing topless around the pool which again any young male studs would notice. Once, we even accompanied them down to the local village coffee shop that also did a very tasty meze. Again, they got plenty of attention from not only the local young lads but the old men too.

Then one morning, around 7:30am, one of the girls, dressed in a very skimpy short nightie that barely covered her modesty, had knocked on our door and said, 'We need you in our bedroom, Mick.'

'Wow what an invitation, but don't tell Phyl,' I muttered even though Phyl was nearby and handed me a large empty yogurt pot and had had a good idea Harry had given them a visit.

'No, it's not like that, Mick, but we do need you in our bedroom,' replied the young lass.

I shot round and saw the other young girl was cowering under the covers of one of the beds. Then I saw Harry. He looked terrifying to any person who didn't know him as he was massive and had got into the girls' bedroom. I had met Harry loads of times and luckily he had never given me any problems. All I needed to get Harry out of the bedroom was an empty yogurt pot to place over him as he was on the wall above the poor girl's bed. Yes, Harry was the name we had given to a big hairy tarantula spider and although Cypriot tarantulas looked scary they are harmless.

Often, on numerous other occasions, I would come home and see an empty yogurt pot upside down on the floor and knew damn well what was underneath. Phyl was good at catching the Harrys but left me to take them out to the undergrowth at the back of our house.

Another time, another Harry was on the wall outside the door of the guest apartment. It was when Bev and Steve from Scarborough were staying and we all had just returned from seeing the *Jersey Boys* at the amphitheatre at Tala. This Harry took off at great speed and ran down the wall and onto the swimming pool. I think he must have been related to Jesus because he didn't float or swim, he ran across the pool water with ease. Bev wanted a photo and Steve was splashing water at him to make it move near to the edge of the pool. Once he was near, Bev said to me, 'Mick, put your finger near his head. I want a photo to show how massive he is, to send to my son.'

'Why my finger?' I asked.

Well, my finger looked tiny in comparison to this big hairy monster but I knew Harry wouldn't be a threat to me.

Paphos Writers' Group

For years, well, OK, about 35 years, I had told many folk that one day I would write a book about my life as a farrier and my life in general. The idea was put into my head by an old client I had known from the day I started work as Derek Spence's apprentice in 1964. He was called Mr John Hawesworth. John became my own client when I started in business on my own a few years later (in my first book I explained Derek had stopped shoeing horses to concentrate on his other business interests). John was a very successful and well-known scriptwriter for television for the many plays and dramas he had written. One series was the '70s drama, *Upstairs, Downstairs*, which I know he had big success with.

Anyway, one day while shoeing John's horses, we were chatting about this and that that what had happened at other stable yards. I can remember there was a bit of scandal at the time at one establishment, and he just said to me, 'Mick, I bet you could write a blooming good book about your life as a farrier.'

So it was John who gave me the idea and he also gave me some good advice. It was to write down any ideas that came into my head and to always have a pen and notebook ready to make a note. I had noticed over the years he was always scribbling down ideas and once told me he had notebook next to his bed as he often woke up from a dream that gave him ideas. If it was left for later, the dream he had had would more than likely be forgotten about by the time morning came. He was right there, the times I had had an idea for a story and didn't write it down. I thought I would remember that and make a note later when I got home. Then, days later, I would be racking my brains trying to remember what I first thought of. So, yes, over the years I did have plenty of one-line prompts that was enough to fill several books, but I had no idea when my first book would ever get started.

I don't know how many people over the years I had told that one day I was going to write a book since John put the idea into my head. Probably about 57000 times, well it felt like I had. Then, the 57001st person was the wrong person to tell, but turned out to be the right one. He was called Maurice Holloway, who was temporary chairman of Paphos Writers' Group. I knew Maurice from other functions we used to attend but I didn't know he was a member of a writers' group. We were having a chat about this and that, when he had said he had got to get home to write that week's topic for the groups meeting, seeing he was temporary chairman. That was when I said, 'One day I am going to write a book about my farrier life.'

Yes, Maurice became the 57001st person and said, 'Well, Mick, in that case I will expect to see you at our group meeting tomorrow morning. It's no good just talking about it.'

I thought, *oh God, I know I said I wanted to write a book but I didn't mean today*, like I had thought for the last 35 odd years. Then again, I was never sure which tomorrow it would be either. At home it didn't help when Phyl told me I must go as Maurice was going to be expecting me. I tried to get out of it by saying these members would be accomplished writers and that I was not sure Maurice would have meant what he said.

The truth was I had only talked about it because I had no idea how to go about writing a book. At the time, I hardly knew how to work a computer. When I left school in the early '60s, my English grammar was terrible, spelling even worse. If I had to write an essay for my English teacher, my attempt would have finished after half a page.

I know I had plenty of one-line prompts but I was not too sure that I would be able to expand them to be counted as a book. Mind you, I would have loved to have seen the expression on my old English teacher's face if I told her all those years ago that I would write a book one day. I think she would have had a good bet that it was beyond my capabilities, and I might have agreed with her at the time. Yes, I needed a good shove and I quote what my old school metalwork teacher used to say: 'There is no such word as can't,' which prompted me to attend my first writers' group meeting that next morning.

That first meeting was not too bad apart from me thinking how I would be able to compete with a room full of folk who have written some amazing stories. Maurice had told me I wouldn't be too involved that morning but just to listen to the readings on that week's topic. I thought, *well at least I will not be making a fool of myself on my first writers' group meeting.* The two-hour session seemed to fly by. There was one or two writing terms I never heard of but nothing like good old

Google for me to look things up at home. When that first meeting came to an end, somebody mentioned the next week's topic was to write a short of story of 850 words about a young child and an animal. Then I heard, 'That includes you, Mick.'

My mind suddenly cast me back to several decades ago when I was in an English lesson at school. Writing a fiction subject essay often ended in disaster. My mind didn't seem to have any imagination then. What made matters worse was my classmate who I sat next to could write forever. I tried to get an idea from his essay but I had a problem. His writing was like a scribble and I couldn't read it. If I had been given the subject of the writer's group when at school, it may have gone something like this.

Little Jimmy's family had got a dog called Fido. He loved that dog and so did his mum and dad. He often went for walks in the woods and along the river bank with Fido. Fido lived until he was 14 and died. The end.

My imagination seemed to be non-existent then. I would never have thought to write what happened on the walks. What breed of dog Fido was, or if Fido was a puppy or a stray when he came into Jimmy's life. I could have described the woods and the river and many other things. I suppose in my young mind, I had to write that Jimmy had a dog. Not about the woods and river or if the animal was young or an older stray when Jimmy got his dog.

For this first topic for the writers' group, I wrote out in longhand as I hardly knew how to work a computer. I knew how to switch one on but I never had an interest in them (I had always left the computer side of things to Phyl). When I wrote my attempt out in long hand, and that felt awkward too. I had never had to write anything like this since I was a teenager. I think the last time I did proper writing was when I took my farrier exam many years ago. How the hell do you write? I felt I had forgotten how to write and would my writing turn out to be like my school classmates scribble. For the last 40-odd years my writing was mostly receipts. Now I needed to read what I had written. I didn't want to have to keep stopping to try to decipher what I had written in front of a room full of accomplished writers, if I ever managed a story. Well, I did write about a child and an animal. I surprised myself and filled two sides of an A4 sheet of paper. That was an achievement as I was worried my story would be like all the others and finish after half a page. I had only guessed 850 words and found my story about the same length as the others. Believe it or not, I could read my own writing.

I must confess, before I read my effort out at the writers' group meeting, I thought it best to read it to Phyl and Ann, a friend, at home. I thought if I was to make a fool of myself, I would rather do it at home first rather than in front of accomplished writers. When I finished, I asked, 'What do you think?'

'It got me welling up,' replied Phyl.

'What, is it that bad?' I muttered thinking the worst.

'No, it's got me welling up with the emotion you have captured,' was her reaction, which I was not expecting.

Now I went off to the writers' group feeling I had written a bestselling novel even though it was only 850 words. Also, I got very good feedback from fellow writers. This was the tomorrow I had waited 35 years for, and it got me started on my goal to write my first book, *All clenched up and nearly finished*. I did buy my own computer and learned what was needed on how to set up all the jargon that is needed to be known about what goes into writing a book.

I now cast my mind back to my school days when Mr Edwards, my metalwork teacher, told me there wasn't such a word as "can't". At the time, my English teacher probably thought "can't" was a word in my case. I think she would have put good money on me that I would never write a book and at the time I might have agreed with her. Now I think of the times Mr Edwards told me there was no such word as can't. He was right. The impossible did happen in my case, but it just took 35 years for the miracle to happen.

GARY AND LINDA

I had got to know Gary, a jobbing builder (not the one who renovated our home), not long after we moved from Chlorikas our first Cypriot home to Koili in 2006. He lived in the village with his wife, Linda, who was Cypriot. Over the years Gary had often done odd jobs for me and took an interest in my life as a farrier. He kept telling me one day he would love to spend a day out with me on my rounds. I had told him that my round extended over the border into the Turkish side and en route I had a client who owned a horse and was a senior person who worked in the UN department in the buffer zone at the old, now-deserted Nicosia airport. This person I will call Ann had a horse which she kept in some outbuildings on the edge of the runway which had been abandoned since the outbreak of the conflict in 1974 between the Greeks and Turks. I knew Gary once told me he worked for the UN but I didn't realise it was at Nicosia and that was when he met Linda, who lived there at the time. When I told him I had an appointment with a client in the UN zone, he asked if he could come with me as he wanted to see what had changed in the years since he left. I told him to remember to bring his passport as we would need it twice. One was to get into the buffer zone and then when we crossed the border on to the Turkish side to go to

Di's stables near Kyrenia. Entering the UN buffer zone, we had to have permission so I had to inform the horse client that Gary was helping me as I did when John came with me.

That day with Gary was the day we got to see inside the old airport terminal building. He just mentioned to the horse owner that he too used to work there when he was a member of the UN. When I had got the horse shod, we were taken for a tour of the airport terminal. Although it was very modern and new in 1974, it was now in a derelict state and nothing had been tampered with or touched since. Also there is an old Cyprus Airways plane standing in the same place, ever since the last passengers disembarked in 1974. Gary told me he remembered stories that he had got told about that aircraft landing. It had had no choice but to land as it was too late to be diverted elsewhere as war had just broken out. Luckily all the passengers did get off it safely. Years later I saw a documentary on television and the pilot of that same aircraft gave an interview and echoed exactly what Gary had told me. He also mentioned about countless businesses that got abandoned, again in the buffer zone.

On the way out, Gary pointed out to me an old 1940s wagon that was hoisted onto a flat roof of a building to advertise the company's business and to this day is still there. Again, in a derelict state. Then there were cars that were new in 1974 still in now-derelict showrooms. Lots, although a little dusty, but still in one piece and are probably worth more now than when they were new.

There were houses with crockery still on tables. Clothes still hanging in wardrobes which had not been touched since the occupiers had to up and leave quickly.

At Famagusta there were several deserted hotels in the buffer zone, many with bullet holes.

In the years that I had been a farrier, I had never expected to be asked into those sensitive regions that were controlled in the aid of peace. I only felt comfortable writing this story since various television documentaries have shown a lot more of what goes on. I think at the time I was just shown what I was allowed to see.

VALENTINE

On evening, Phyl and I were out for a meal at a little restaurant when my mobile rang. It was from another farrier who I had heard of but never met. His name was Valentine and he was asking for my advice. The horse in question had very bad cracked hooves and he had the idea I may be able to help. Valentine came from Bulgaria and had lived in Cyprus for a few years working as a farrier. He was different from the Cypriot farriers and was not afraid to ask for an opinion if he didn't know how to tackle a problem. He had got lots of knowledge of horses, not just shoeing them – he was an accomplished rider too. I had heard he got good results from schooling as well. He was the type of guy that if he wanted advice, he was not afraid to ask and was always willing to learn. His farrier skills were what he had picked up over the years and I must say his work looked quite good. Well, it was a lot better than other "fully qualified farriers" who had done a two-month course and knew everything. Well, the guy who knows everything has not been born yet. Valentine would look at his work and he would often say, 'Could I have shod the horse better?' Well, in my eyes, Valentine was always looking for improvement and could he have done the job better. He is not alone in that department because I used to think the same. In life they can always be someone better.

Well, as I say, this phone call caught me off guard as he wanted me to go with him to one of his client's horses that had got big sand cracks in both front hooves. I agreed to meet up later that following week and I found if you are doing any favour for folk in Cyprus, they want to buy you lunch. Sure enough, that happened when he met up with me. I had had horses to shoe on a yard just outside Limassol and I told him I would be finished around midday. Valentine lived in Nicosia and Limassol was halfway between Koili, near Paphos, and Nicosia. That is another thing about local folk in Cyprus – they were never in a hurry and Valentine insisted on buying me lunch and having a chat. He told me his lady friend at the time had relations in the UK and he had stayed with her sister who had studied at Loughborough University. I told him I used to live in a village a short distance from Loughborough. Valentine looked surprised and said, 'Do you know a farrier called Phil Humphrey, I once spent a day with him when I visited the in-laws.'

'I know Phil very well,' I replied and then one story led to another and before we knew it an hour and half had passed.

I couldn't believe meeting a guy from Bulgaria living in Cyprus with his Cypriot lady friend and we end up talking about folk we both know back in the UK. The world is a small place.

Finally, we thought we had better make a move to have a look at Valentine's client's horse with the foot problem. I thought I was just going to be giving my opinion but, no, I ended shoeing two horses with full sets of shoes. The one with the problem had got a massive sand crack at the toe of both front hooves.

Luckily, they didn't come down from the coronet band but up from the foot surface. I have explained how in Cyprus bog-standard horseshoes are fitted and this was the case here. The horse's owner said that the horse also tripped when ridden. The shoes that had being fitted had the clip smack bang in the middle of the sand crack and was forcing the crack to get wider. All I did was to knock the clip off the front of the shoes and roll the toe of the shoe to help the break over. Again, when I got an inch of toe off the crack didn't look half as bad. Then the owner asked, 'Can you put the hind shoes on and shoe the other, Mick?'

I looked at Valentine because the last thing I wanted to do was to pinch his work and he said, 'Well, Mick, if you have got time, why not.'

Valentine didn't want me just to sort out problems with his clients' horses but his own too. I remember one young horse he had dragged its hind feet and had worn the toe of the shoe to non-existence and rounded off the hoof too. He had watched me on the horse that had the sand crack and saw how easy it was to roll the toe of the shoe from having a gas forge. He thought his own young horse would benefit from a roll on its hind shoes. He wanted me to inspect his attempt to roll the toes of the shoe. I was puzzled even though he done a decent job and I asked, 'How the hell did you roll the toes without a forge?'

'With a blow lamp and the edge of a concrete block although it took an age to get the shoe hot,' Valentine replied.

He also saw the benefits that came with a gas forge and how alterations or modifications could be done to make horseshoeing better and easier. He had looked into buying his own when I found that one of my customers had one plus an anvil. Valentine asked me if they would be willing to sell and I managed to negotiate a price which he accepted. How I saw Valentine was that he didn't want to just slap four shoes on a horse, he wanted the horse to be shod with a little more quality.

Another time, he got me to go and look at a horse with very bad laminitis. Again, it was at Nicosia and when I saw it I thought it needed to lose a good 1cwt or more in weight. It was massive and when I found out what it had been fed on, I could understand why. I tried to tell the owner she was killing it by trying to be too kind but really she had being cruel feeding it too much rich food. Sometimes in these cases one has to be a little bit cruel to be kind and cut out all titbits and any animal food that contains molasses.

I have often told the lady owners over the years to treat their animals the same way they would treat their husband. They all used to say, 'We would never treat our horses that bad.'

Also, the vet didn't seem to know what to do even though she tried to give the impression she did. I had a good idea the pedal bone had rotated to be sticking through the soles of both front hooves and I was sure it needed a resection to relieve the pressure of the infection. It had a raging pulse and hooves that were very hot. Also, it was standing back on its heels and rocking like a rocking horse. I think any horse person would have diagnosed laminitis. I found out the vet had nerve blocked both front hooves to check if the problem was even in the hooves.

I had to keep giving this vet instructions as to what I wanted to do. For a start, could she give the animal a bit of sedation to help while I worked on it? I managed to trim a load of hoof off after a fashion with the help of Valentine as the horse couldn't stand very well even sedated. Also, we managed to do a resection to try to relieve pressure from the throbbing horse's foot. The vet said she wanted a bar shoe on but her bar shoes were going to be very different to what I had in my mind. She wanted me to fit raised bar shoes which was the last thing the horse would want. Raised bar shoes would help to push the pedal bone further through its soles. What was needed was heart bar shoes which are flat and shaped like a heart. I had to draw her a little diagram of what would happen if we went with her idea. Then she agreed with me and tried to tell the owner why the horse needed heart bar shoes as if it was her idea.

I had a good idea this horse was not going to stand or be able to bear me nailing heart bar shoes on. I came up with a solution to tape a pair on. It was a little bit of improvising with what we had. Deep down, I had a feeling it might be a lost cause. In my first book I told of a case of a horse in the same predicament in the UK, although that one wasn't too overweight and I had a top vet to work with who really knew his job. Now I felt I had to tell the vet what to do instead of the vet telling me.

A week later, the owner got in touch to thank me for what I had done. She told me she had tried another vet as the lady vet she had used seemed unsure what to do next. The second one didn't know either and suggested it may be best if he put the poor thing to sleep. With how much pain that horse was in and suffering, I think I would have agreed but it wasn't my place to say that. Farriers are not supposed to recommend an animal to be put to sleep even if we think it. That is for the owner and vet to discuss although in Cyprus the rules are not like rules in the UK. I have had clients in the UK who tried their best to keep their loving pets alive longer than they should have. That was my opinion though and I wouldn't have mentioned it either. It is too easy to tell someone that their loyal pet should be put to sleep. I think I should have had one or two of my dogs put to sleep when old age caught up with them and when they developed big problems that were not nice to them. They were my friends and I didn't want to lose them. I was trying to keep them alive for me not for them. I know it is a very difficult decision to make when it's your own faithful animal and the last thing I would want is someone who is not a vet to be giving their opinion. I think I may be like others and hope that the diagnoses could be wrong and the animal may recover with medication. So this horse in Cyprus was probably put to sleep for its own good. I think it may have suffered for a long time under the circumstances.

As I have said, Valentine rang me while out one Saturday evening while having a meal at a restaurant with my wife. I had never met him before when he asked me to look at a horse he had problems with. The following Saturday he had driven down from Nicosia and we were having a meal in the same restaurant Phyl and I were in the week before. He was a guy who made you feel you had known him for years.

The couple who owned the restaurant, Colin and Gloria, did home cooked meals like tasty fish pies and many other delicious dishes. I had asked Valentine and his then lady friend if they wanted to go for a local taverna for a meze or Colin and Gloria's.

They surprised me that they chose Colin and Gloria's as they were fed up eating mezes and moussakas. They wanted to try Gloria's homemade fish pies and apple crumble puddings. Well, they were not disappointed as they visited a few months later and we had to go for another meal.

SOCIAL LIFE

While we lived in Cyprus, our social life became hectic in a nice way. There was always someone saying. "We are going to Maria's for Sunday lunch, are you joining us?" Well, Maria had a taverna up in the hills in a little village called Fyti. She was a lovely lady who we got to know before we had bought our first home in Cyprus. I can remember telling her on our first meeting in October 2000 that one day we wanted to live on the island. She was a lady that when you first met, you felt you had known her for years. So, of course, when we moved there full-time her taverna was one of the many places we ate out at.

Also, the fun we had too. I had told her I was learning Greek on my first meeting with her and I was sure I would be fluent the next week. Of course, years later it was always going to be, the next week, and by Jove she never let me forget it even though I could order drinks in broken Greek. She used to say to other diners, 'Do you know how long he's been telling me he will be fluent in Greek? I bet it's over ten years and it is always the next week when he will be fluent.'

'But I'll be fluent next week, Maria,' I would butt in with a cheeky reply.

Another time we were with John and Gill and Maria asked if she could get us more drink. John and I had had a beer and John said, 'Maria, this beer bottle seems to have a hole in it and the beer has leaked out.'

'Where is the hole, John?' she said while holding the bottle up and looking at the bottom of it.

'The other end, Maria. All the beer leaked out when I poured it into my glass and now my glass is empty and that seems to have a bigger hole in it.'

'I was just about to get you another free one thinking I had given you a dodgy bottle, John,' she replied with a laugh.

'Oh, I don't mind a free one,' he said in a cheeky voice.

Maria's taverna was a really relaxing place either to eat out or just calling in for a coffee! She made time to welcome everyone. Not only that, no matter what meal you ordered, it could be from a full meze to tuna salad, they all tasted delicious.

BEV

When I asked Bev if she minded if I wrote a little something about her, she said as long it wasn't on page three with a sexy photo of her. I said to her with in a mischievous way, 'If you had wanted page three, Bev, with a photo, I would personally have to take the shot.' So that is why she is on page 190 and not in a scantily dressed pose.

I got introduced to Bev and her husband, John, when I did work for the donkey sanctuary outreach program. They lived in a village near to Zygi in Cyprus. Over several years I had looked after Bev and John's donkeys even after stopping doing work for the donkey sanctuary. I got the feeling she trusted me more than the others who pretended to be farriers and she paid me to attend to her donkeys privately. Her donkeys were of a friendly nature and they seemed to appreciate the fuss and love Bev and John had not only for their donkeys but their dogs too. She told me years later, the farrier before me seemed nervous when he attended. Well, if he was nervous with them I dread to think what he was like with a frisky-natured one. These were some of the easiest animals to work with.

As we got to know each other, there was always a little bit of what I call "polite cheeky banter". After the donkeys had had their feet manicured, Bev insisted we had to drink a cup of her lovely tea. This is when I found Bev could take this "cheeky banter" but give it too. The laughs and happy atmosphere with clients like Bev I found over the years made either shoeing horses or trimming donkey feet easier.

It wasn't as if I was in a rush to get to the next call like when I was in business in the UK. My work was only part-time although some days I may have thought differently. So often I wasn't rushed of my feet and I had time to stop for a drink and natter with Bev and John.

Their property consisted of their house and a garage where John, a mechanic, repaired cars, and a small barn made into stables which led to a paddock. Bev and John worshiped their donkeys Madam, Holly, and Kirk and of course their dogs too. Their animals lived a life of Riley. I am sure all their animals got spoilt with lots of love and kindness, rather than too many treats which could have given the donkeys health problems. Both of them loved their animals and talked to them as if they were human. I had always spoken to my dogs the same way and I am sure animals can understand, perhaps better than talking to a fellow human. With Bev and John, I don't think they had a favourite, all their animals were favourites to them.

Bev's donkeys were a pleasure to trim every two months or so. Even after two months, they never looked desperate and with it just being straightforward trims we were soon sitting in Bev and John's kitchen drinking mugs of tea! I found my farrier life in Cyprus to be done at a slower pace than the UK. I suppose that, not expecting to work again, the job became more like a hobby, unlike in the UK where I hadn't got time to stop for tea breaks. I hadn't intended to make a living from farrier work in Cyprus, but I must confess I did very well from working just two or three days a week.

While drinking Bev's tea we would put the world right and talked about other amusing things that had happened to us. John, who was an English Cypriot, told us of the tale when he worked in a large garage. He told me about a bloke who had a problem with his car who drove into the garage. The customer spoke in broken English and very slowly and in loud voice like you do when you think that others wouldn't understand you. The conversation went something like this: 'Red IGNITION LIGHT ON. YOU FIX.'

'LIFT BONNET,' John said back in a slow, loud voice and motioning with his arms for the motorist to lift the bonnet. 'I CHECK ALTERNATOR. I THINK ALTERATOR NOT CHARGING, NO GOOD, KAPUT,' John replied in the same dialogue, loud and slow.

'NO GOOD. YOU FIX,' again the guy asked.

'NO GOOD NEW ONE I FIX,' John replied again in a Dalek-type voice.

The phone rings and another colleague shouts in perfect English, 'John, you are wanted on the phone.'

'OK I will be there in a minute,' he shouted back in perfect English.

The customers whose car that needed a new alternator, looked at John and said in perfect English when he heard John answer his workmate, 'I thought you didn't speak English, that's why I spoke slow and loud. Why the hell are we talking like this?'

'I thought you didn't speak English either,' replied John.

Yes, it was a pleasure doing work for Bev and John and I was delighted she wanted me to trim her donkey's hooves after I left the donkey sanctuary. I looked after her donkey's right up until she decided to return to the UK, which included shipping all her beloved animals back with her.

PAT'S RIDING SCHOOL

When Pat popped her head over the stable door at George's Ranch, I thought she was just stabling her horse there at the time. It never entered my head that one day she would take over the running of a riding school at Aphrodite Hills. Aphrodite Hills consisted of a hotel and a golf club surrounded by very expensive villas. Although Aphrodite Hills was at the top of a steep hill, the riding school was situated away from the main part of the resort down a long, unmade road. The first time I went to shoe Pat's horses, I thought I had misheard the directions as this unmade road seemed to go on for miles. I had started to think I ought to give her a ring as I was sure I had done a wrong turn somewhere. I was just about to give up when I spotted some buildings out in the sticks and sure enough this was Pat's riding school. Although it's a long bumpy car ride to the riding school, it is perfect for horseback riders who want to hack out away from the busy road traffic. The land and stables were owned by the Aphrodite Hills hotel and lots of Pat's clients were holidaymakers who enjoyed horse riding. When I was there shoeing the horses there was always a steady flow of folk coming for lessons or hacks out.

One of the first horses I shod for Pat was Mac, who she had brought with her from the UK. He was the one I gave a foot trim to the morning Pat had poked her head over the stable door at George's Ranch. Although he was never a problem to me shoeing-wise, he would like to swing his bottom onto the stable for a good rub due to sweet itch. Whatever remedy Pat administered didn't seem to work and I could understand how it must have caused Mac discomfort. Sweet itch can affect some horses whereas others never suffer from it. I didn't blame Mac when he decided on a good rub on the stable wall for relief. The biggest job was he took some shifting. Mind you, he was fine while I was fitting his shoes, it was when I let go he soon swung his back end for a good scratch on the stable.

The second one was a young horse that Pat had the chance to buy and was called Bonnie. Before committing to buying Bonnie, Pat was worried about a problem on the hind legs. I was confident that a little change to how it had got shod before would work in its favour, seeing as Bonnie was a young horse. Unfortunately, although I did help with the conformation of Bonnie's hind legs and she was good for me to shoe, she was a bit unpredictable to ride. Bonnie was still a youngster and everybody thought she may change with age. I have seen the same situation over the years and although some do get better behaved, lots don't. Sadly, Bonnie, from what I understand, was a horse getting worse rather than better behaved to ride. Then one day while Pat was out riding, there was the sound of gunshot in the distance and Bonnie bolted. OK, lots of animals would have done the same but Pat got thrown off with her foot caught in the stirrup. After time off with a serious injury to her leg, she felt there was no way could she let other riders on Bonnie so she got sold on!

Another of the liveries was a horse called Snowy, who I had first shod at George's Ranch. At the time I had never met Snowy's owner, who was called Sandy. When Snowy was at livery at George's Ranch, the staff told me not to do too much dressing of Snowy's hooves as it could make him lame. I asked why and was told the Cypriot farrier had told them he dare not trim too much off because Snowy would go lame if he did. I had a very different opinion. The first time I saw him it looked as if the horse was walking with flip-flops on. I noticed the shoes that had been fitted were all embedded in his hooves and all the clenches were so low that some were nearly touching the shoe. My first thought was a blooming good foot trim would help. I thought, *he is going to be lame if he is left with toes that are way too long.*

Once I had trimmed loads of overgrown toe off, I decided to use a wide web shoe. I also seated out the shoe just in case he didn't like any pressure on his soles, but I didn't think Snowy had that problem. When I nailed on, he stood perfect. Also his hooves didn't look so flat-footed. I did get the groom to trot him out just to make sure I wasn't wrong with my diagnosis. To my relief he trotted out sound as a bell. When I did meet Snowy's owner, she told me she couldn't believe her eyes and that her horse had normal feet (the Cypriot farrier who used to attend to Snowy was the one who told me he was "the best farrier in

Cyprus"). So now Snowy became my client and had moved into the livery at Pat's.

Claire, who gave riding tuition at Pat's riding school, asked me if I would go with her for my opinion on a horse she was interested in called Nacho. Nacho was only a five-year-old and as soon as I saw him I felt sorry for how and where he had got to live. He was tethered out in the open and in the full sun. I think Claire felt sorry for him too. I suppose it is often the normal way things are done in Cyprus. Regardless of this, Nacho looked in fine form and the only thing I could see that was bit of a problem was his hind legs. He was unshod and his hooves turned in. As soon as I picked a hind foot up, I could see why he turned them in. The inside of the hind feet were overgrown, and the outside were short. I had helped many a horse over the years with the same problem by putting a road non-slip stud (plug) with a tungsten pin insert in the shoe near to the quarter clip instead of the heel. This helped not only to stop the horse slipping on the road but helped the shoe to wear more evenly. Some farriers would put a non-slip nail, but I found that the tungsten pin often broke off.

Claire did buy Nacho and I knew she would give him a more comfortable way of life and what a star he turned out to be. The first time I shod him at the side of Claire's home was under a tree. Yes, I was under any type of shade in Cyprus to shield me from the hot sun. Although I didn't think he'd been shod before, my gut feeling was that I didn't expect any problems when I fitted his first set of shoes. My gut feeling was right, Nacho was a perfect client and stood perfectly considering the conditions, and this time it wasn't just the hot unbearable sunshine. Although I was grateful of the shade from the hot sun, when I began to shoe Nacho a thunderstorm erupted just as I was about to nail his new shoes on. The weather changed from a sunny day into a big thunder and lightning storm in less than half an hour after I arrived. The cracks of thunder were so loud and the strikes of lightning were flashing a little too close for comfort and to make matters worse, we were sheltering under a tree. Nacho just carried on eating from his hay net and although the heavens had opened up the tree provided the shelter as none of us got wet. OK, probably a bit damp but not soaked to the skin. Then again, in Cyprus, some days I would have gladly stood out in the rain to cool down.

After several shoeings, the road stud plugs had worked a treat and Nacho had started to move his hind limbs straighter. A year or so later, Nacho had come to live at Pat's stables and was perfect for folk who were novice riders. Claire had done lots of teaching at Pat's and now Nacho was the perfect horse for teaching Pat's clients, and he became a big favourite too.

Carmen, a mare, was a horse Pat had been given for free due to foot problems. This mare came from the stables owned by a husband and wife where I made the Shire shoes for George. How it was explained to me was that when Carmen was ridden, it felt as if she had got a puncture on one of her hooves but George and others didn't seem to know which one. Before I shod, I got Pat to trot Carmen out. I could see the shoes on the front looked miles too small but I didn't think it was the front end where the problem was. The times I have watched horsey folk only look for a lameness when the horse is trotted towards them and never take a note of the horse's rear end when trotted away. If the horse is observed from its rear when trotted away from you, the problem sometimes is easier to detect. That was when I realised what was wrong. Carmen's near hind hoof heels needed raising. Not how they had got trimmed but more what Carmen was born with. It would be like a human walking with a heel on one shoe and not on the other.

I shod with a normal set of shoes and put a little plastic wedge under the heel of the near hind shoe and the difference that made was unbelievable. She didn't trot as if she got a puncture I was told later. Carmen went on to teach many of Pat's clients to ride for many more years. I was told she was another big favourite too for beginners who needed a bit more confidence.

I think Pat once mentioned to Carmen's last owner how I got Carmen sound. Pat was told she was lucky to have me as her farrier. The other owner said they were stuck with George. I felt a big-headed when Pat told me what the husband and wife had said about me. When some of those Cypriot farriers have said they are fully qualified they have got it into their heads that they have nothing more to learn. George had told me he had got fully qualified after a three-month course abroad. I never found out which country he qualified in, but it certainly wasn't the UK.

Pat phoned me one evening to see if I could go and give my opinion on a new livery that had arrived at her stables that was not sound. The next morning, I called in and although she had a good idea what this pony's problems may be, it wasn't hard to diagnose acute laminitis. By what I was told, it had once been a top gymkhana pony. The owners had bought it for their then 14-year-old son who was a very good rider with potential. Unfortunately, the lad's parents, although wanted the best for their son, were not horsey folk. All they knew was this pony had won many competitions that it had entered. Anybody who was around horse's day in and day out would have seen that this pony was a few stone overweight. The withers were huge and the hooves were hot, plus had a raging pulse.

I advised them to call Yiannis the vet. I had started to do more work other than the donkey sanctuary with Yiannis and I got him to X-ray the hooves first. I had a good idea the X-rays would show a result we didn't want to see. Sure enough, they did. The pedal bones in both front feet had rotated and were ready to poke through the sole. I said to Yiannis we needed to put heart bar shoes on. At the time he had never heard of heart bar shoes, and I had to explain how they worked to him. He was a good listener and he told Pat that I was more up to date with the latest treatment for laminitis. After all, she had known me for many years and mentioned to him about my track record in the UK. That is not to say Yiannis was a bad vet. He had only worked with smaller animals before he got involved with the donkey sanctuary and he wanted to broaden his skills. I still needed Yiannis's help as I couldn't do X-rays or administer drugs or medication although I had a good idea what might be needed.

This young lad's parents, although they knew nothing about horses or ponies, did everything that was asked to help to get their son's pony better. I refitted the heart bar shoes every four weeks instead of six weeks. When a horse has laminitis, the hoof growth accelerates and the last thing you want to happen is the toe to get too long and the heels too high.

I know I had got good results from bad laminitis cases with horses and ponies in the UK, but I had worked with top vets. Many times in Cyprus, I felt I should have qualified as a vet although the equine veterinary did improve over time. Yiannis did once say lots of vets had never specialised in equine and he knew he had got lots to learn. This pony did recover and when it lost its excessive weight it looked a different pony from that first day I had set eyes on it.

Another client, Wendy, had bought a horse which I understood could have been looked after a little better by its previous owners. The horse was unshod with hooves maybe a little overgrown and chipped, which gave Wendy a little cause to be concerned. I didn't see any issue farrier-wise as I had seen a lot worse. I had shod horses that were in a worse state than this one and never gave it another thought. In fact, when I got Wendy's horse fitted with new shoes its feet didn't look half as bad. I have often thought a well shod horse or hooves that are trimmed neat and tidy can look to change the outlook on the condition of the animal. I would like to think that is what happened in this case. It had nice round open feet that any farrier would have liked if it was one in a farrier competition. Six weeks later, when I was called for its next set, there was not a hint of any of the chips and cracks from when I first shod it. All the time the horse was stabled at Pat's, that horse never gave me any trouble shoeing-wise.

Wendy then moved to other stables and got a new farrier. I think she spent more time not able to ride due to lost shoes. I heard she was told the reason why her horse lost so many shoes was because the hooves were not good. I did think it odd that same horse had good strong hooves when I shod it, could now be having problems. I was shown photos later and could see the problem. It was all to do with the dressing of the feet before fitting the shoes.

Another pony I had the pleasure to shoe was Troy, owned by Emily and her mum, Helen. They both competed with Troy and other horses at many horse shows. Over the years, Troy had never given me trouble until I went on holiday to the UK. While I was on holiday for a month, Troy needed to be shod and another farrier who was on standby for me (not Anglos) shod him. A week or so after I returned, Emily asked me why her horse was lame for a few days after the other guy had shod him and had never had a problem before. She said she was always able to ride straight after but on this occasion she couldn't for a few days. Although he did get better a few days later, my first thought was nail bind. This is when the farrier has got the nail pressing on sensitive tissue rather than in sensitive tissue. When Emily described it to me, I thought that it could get better on its own without the shoe being taken off. I am sure all farriers have had this happen to them and it is very easy on a bad-footed or an awkward horse. Mind you, if a farrier says it's never happened to them, I would suspect they are telling a lie or they have not shod many bad-footed, bad-tempered horses. I think all of us have caught one now and then unintentionally, but Troy was not difficult to shoe.

When I did see the job on Troy, I had a good idea the nailing on was fine and even the fitting. What I did notice was the shoe looked to be fitted very tight on the sole. I was always taught to give a sliver of a clearance between the sole and shoe. If the sole is thin seat the shoe out. Make sure the pressure of the shoe is on the outer wall of the hoof rather than on the sole. So for all the years I shod horses, I did that on every horse I had shod naturally.

There were many other horses and ponies that Pat had at her stables. Some in livery but I found it a busy but happy place to work. There was always a constant stream of clients of many different nationalities. Lots who were her regular clients lived in Cyprus but many who were holidaying not just at the Aphrodite hotel but from other holiday resorts. Many came back year after year to ride in the beautiful unspoilt rugged terrain of Cyprus.

Marlene's riding school

I first got to know Marlene when she asked me to trim a horse's hooves which she had just taken on loan. It was at a time when I hadn't quite quit the donkey sanctuary and thought any horsey work that came my way I would accept. I don't know how Marlene had heard about me or got hold of my mobile number but I knew my name seemed to getting talked about the length and breadth of Cyprus. I had arranged to trim Marlene's horse's feet on the way home from the donkey sanctuary. John was with me on this first appointment. Marlene had her friend there who owned a pet shop called Shampooch at Yeroskipou who also did dog grooming. Both were very friendly and seemed to like a bit of humour as soon as we got out of my van. I thought this was a good sign as it is part of most farrier's DNA as we like a good laugh and a happy atmosphere to work in. I think any business that encourages this gets more out of staff and work done more efficiently. With me, I couldn't seem to miss a chance for a little bit of mischievous leg pulling.

Although Marlene was concerned about the length of the horse's hooves, she asked if I could see anything of concern. I knew it was not her fault for the state the nag's feet as she had just taken delivery of it on a loan. Over in Cyprus, there is an awful lot of laminitis cases and Marlene was worried that this horse hadn't got the symptoms. I could see why she was concerned as it was grossly overweight and needed overdue attention to its overgrown hooves.

'The feet are fine,' I said after I had gone round twice with my nippers on each foot and looked back to how they should be.

'They do look better, Mick. I was worried what you were going to say when you saw they hadn't seen a farrier for a long time,' replied Marlene.

'The only thing I can see wrong, apart from the horse needing to go on a diet, is it has two left feet,' I said with John agreeing.

'Two left feet? We never spotted that,' came the startled reply from both women.

'You mean you didn't know?' both myself and John informed them with a serious look on our faces.

Now both women were standing in front of the horse and looking down at the front hooves.

'Here, come and stand sideways on and you will see what we mean,' I muttered.

'What are we looking at?' came the reply.

'Surely you can see it now. One left foot at the front and one at the back and you two didn't know?' I said with a mischievous look.

Both of them did laugh when they realised I was having a joke at their expense. Although they looked as if they could have hit me, I knew they both loved a bit of mischievous banter.

Months past and Marlene bought another horse of her own and now wanted shoes on both horses that were doing more work. At her home she had a couple of stables built plus a full-size sand school. A year later she had bought land up in the hills just outside a village called Amargeti. Perfect for horse riding. Over a period of time on this land, Marlene had built around a dozen stables and two or three barns, wash and shower room, toilets and a club house. Not to mention two ménages. What was once a bare field had become a nicely landscaped, and built-to-perfection, beautiful block of stables! She had even thought of a covered stand with a concrete base which was perfect for any farrier. By now she had acquired many more horses and some at livery too. I used to shoe half one day and the rest a fortnight later.

The other thing was a million or more flies seemed to like the Cyprus climate. They were a pain for any animal and humans too. It didn't seem to matter what lotions or potions were tried. It was the same on a hot day in the UK – they could make a horse, especially the thoroughbreds or for that matter a human, fidget. They were my biggest pest no matter which stables I was working at. It didn't seem to matter what fly repellent was used but it only seemed to work for a minute before they were back. Marlene had other ideas though. Where I shod her horses, she had erected two big powerful fans. That was better than any lotion or potion that was supposed to keep these irritating insects away. I think any that dared to fly in soon got blasted back out. Also the fans made the very hot climate more comfortable to work in and I am sure the horses enjoyed it too.

I really enjoyed doing work for Marlene. One of her horses, Babalou, she had acquired for her riding school did give me a little cause for concern on the first shoeing. It didn't look sound to me but I was hoping it was just how it had got shod before. To me, the toe of its hooves looked again to be far too long. When I inspected it, I found the last farrier had left a stack of growth on the toe and had fitted the shoes far too big. Usually I found it to be the other way round and not big enough. After I got the foot trimmed to more an acceptable length I saw my worst fear, the first signs of laminitis. Marlene had feared the same and had already started to watch the horse's diet. Luckily, we must have caught the laminitis in time as over the years we never had any issues to cause any concern. From what I can gather, Babalou was her best horse for folk who were just beginners who wanted to learn to ride.

Another day I had finished shoeing and Franz, who came from Holland and did odd jobs for Marlene, had made a brew of tea in the club house for me and a Romanian guy who worked as Marlene's groom. It was when we had stopped for our break Franz asked me if I ever trimmed a pig's trotters. Marlene had a fat belly pig which ran loose around the stable yard. Franz thought its trotters were starting to curl up and needed attention. One thing led to another and the next thing we found the three of us herding the pig back into its pen. I thought it would only take a few minutes and we would soon have its trotters trimmed. Franz was holding onto the pig's head and I found the animal very friendly and it didn't seem to want to put up any fight. That changed as soon as I opened my clippers and squeezed to cut off the excess growth. The animal let out a piercing squeal. I am sure if anybody within a two-mile radius would have heard and thought we were committing a murder. I think we were more startled than the pig as it never struggled once while I trimmed its trotters. It just squealed with an ear-piercing shriek for a full ten minutes or however long it took me. In fact, I don't think it minded me chopping at its overgrown feet. I don't know if the screeching the whole time was to try and frighten us off or what, but it never gave up until we had finished. I don't know who was more stressed, us or the pig.

Other times, on more of social occasions, Marlene put on, usually on a Sunday afternoon, a music show and a barbecue for many of her horsey clients and friends. I can remember that she would book a Dire Straits tribute band. The guys who performed were first-class and although not musicians doing it for a living, they acted very professionally. Also they sounded exactly like the original Dire Straits band.

As for my farrier life in Cyprus, stables like Marlene's and lots of others were a pleasure to do work for. The atmosphere on those sunny, cloudless warm days I think made folk happy to be out and about and to really enjoy functions not only at Marlene's riding school but other establishments too.

COWBOY JOHN

I got introduced to John when I was asked to be duty farrier at a horse show at Episokpi riding club. He had asked me if I would be interested in shoeing his horse. He mentioned that his horse wobbled on its back end when he rode it and hoped I could help to improve its conformation. I made an appointment to have a look to see if I could help with this so called wobble. The farrier before me had only wanted to fit front shoes and never touched the hind. He had never checked to see if they even needed a trim. Before I picked a foot up, I got John to trot his horse out up the road. I could see the hind feet were far from balanced. I knew what I was going to see as soon as I picked its hind feet up. There must have been an inch of growth on the inside of the hoof and none on the outside. I didn't know the reason why the last farrier hadn't checked this. I suspect as John's horse could lean away from you and not on you, the farrier thought it might fall over. I had shod ones a lot worse, so I didn't see that too much of a problem. I know John's old farrier was not the bravest but I didn't class this horse as dangerous. More to do with balance by getting tipped over by an inch of growth on the inside of its hoof.

I asked John if he would mind me fitting shoes all round. On the hind I put my trusted road plug stud near to the side clip on the outside branch of the hind shoes. I had done this on other horses with a similar problem and got good results from something so simple to do. Mind you, in Cyprus lots of these so-called farriers are not really farriers. Some can do a reasonable job if it is straightforward. When it involves punching or drilling stud holes, that becomes a problem. I don't think half of them knew what a road stud was or there were such things as horseshoes for different kinds of lameness.

I shod John's horse and hoped my idea helped. Around a fortnight later, John got in touch and by the tone of his voice as soon as he spoke, I was relieved to hear that my idea had worked wonders. The first words I heard from John were, 'He doesn't wobble any more when I ride.'

That is all I did – put a road stud in the shoe and it improved the horse's action. Also the shoe wore more evenly and the hind hooves grew more level. As time went by, we had both given up asking if the horse was moving better. We both just took it nothing was wrong and had forgotten that we had started with a problem.

I must say, John wasn't called "cowboy" from shady unscrupulous deals but because he enjoyed watching old Western films. Also he did look like a seasoned cowboy when he rode his horse in his Western attire.

He also had a little car hire business and was much cheaper than the many car rental companies. Although his cars were getting on in years, I must say they were kept in better working order than some of the major car rental establishments that had nearly new models. I know as on a few occasions we had hired two or three when relations were visiting us from the UK.

ANN AND JEZ

I find the world to be small no matter which country you are in nowadays. I went on holiday to Tenerife a few years ago and met a horsey client from the UK who happened to be on holiday at the same time. That was the time we had a timeshare holiday apartment. One year, on our arrival, we went to check in and found we had got cancelled. I assured the lady at the reception desk that it wasn't us who had cancelled. On seeing the worried look on our faces, she found us on their computing system and realised we had never cancelled and it was their mistake. She did one or two phone calls and managed to get us alternative accommodation at another nearby timeshare resort. Although this was not as well run as where our own timeshare was, it was fine for a base as we were out all day. We were relieved that this other complex had a room for us.

One day we called in at where we were supposed to be staying. I had gone into the bar and ordered our drinks and was looking for somewhere to sit I heard a women shout, 'Mick!' Not taking any notice, I heard, 'Mick, Mick!' Looking around, thinking it was someone shouting to their other half called Mick, I realised it meant me.

'What a surprise meeting you here, Jenny,' I said with surprised look.

'We decided to swap our timeshare this year to Tenerife,' Jenny muttered.

'Just as a matter of interest, which apartment were you given?' I asked.

'Room number five up there,' she said as she pointed to our room.

'Room five is our apartment. We usually come every year. When we got to check in the other night, we were told we cancelled. Anyway, they got us sorted and we are booked in just up the road.'

I couldn't believe out of all the folk that could have ended up with our room, it had to be an old client of mine. This was one example of how small the world is. It was the same meeting up with Pat and her husband from Leicestershire in Cyprus. Neither of us had any idea we would meet up again in Cyprus to live and who else were we likely to meet.

Well, I didn't have to wait that long before another old client from the UK got in touch. It was Ann and Jez. I had known Ann from the time I had started my own business in 1976. In my first book I had told the story how she helped a farmer friend, called Bill, out with his horses. It would be over 40-odd years ago when Ann had booked me to shoe a four-year-old that belonged to Bill for its first set of shoes. The horse in question, I had no problem trimming its feet on other occasions, and I didn't expect it to be too much of a problem to fit the shoes. How wrong we could be. This time it wouldn't let me get near it to start. We were on the verge of giving up. Then, without any warning, it reared up in the air. I don't know how high it went, maybe seven or eight feet and it seemed to twist its body in mid-air. After landing on its side it struck its head on a machine that dug potatoes out of the ground. It looked still a bit dazed when it got back on its feet and never moved a muscle while I shod it.

Ann, over the years, had looked after and ridden many of Bill's horses and eventually bought her own horse called Lady. She had told me Lady didn't walk straight on the hind feet. She wore the outside branch of the shoe until there was no metal left but the inside branch looked hardly worn. Again, for years before I retired to Cyprus, I shod Lady with an ordinary set of hind shoes with a trusted road stud plug near the outside hind shoe clip. That was all I did and Lady walked much better and the shoe wore more evenly. I shod Lady like this for many years without any issues. She told me that when I left for Cyprus, she had tried several farriers and Lady went back to walking skew-whiff again. She said the other farriers were always in a tearing hurry and hadn't got time to do what I did.

All the time I had known Ann and Jez I never imagined that I would be meeting them in Cyprus one day. I can remember the first phone call I received off Ann to say they were in Cyprus on holiday and could they call in to see us. I never expected them to tell me that they were thinking of coming to Cyprus to live. Well, I always thought that they would stay living in Birstall near Leicester for the rest of their lives. I thought they were never the globetrotting type who had holidays in a foreign country, never mind living in one.

Their first home, which they had rented, was near to the coast between Limassol and Larnaca. If you are not used to the heat this is the last place you would want to live and Ann found the humidity unbearable. One day I had Bev's donkey to trim and she lived not far from where Ann and Jez was staying. Both Phyl and I thought we would give them a call seeing as we were nearby. The night before our planned visit, Ann phoned us to say she was struggling with the heat and they were back in the UK. I thought that was that and their adventure had come to an end.

A few months later we got a call from Ann. They wanted to give Cyprus another go and asked if they could book our apartment for two weeks. They realised that the climate where we lived wasn't as humid as down near the coast. (Before we moved to Koili from Chlorakas I used to joke that I felt wetter than when I was in the shower from sweat). They wanted to see if where we lived made a difference and did we know of any houses to rent.

A few days after they arrived to stay with us, we knew of one house but that was for sale. At the time they didn't want to commit to buying before they were sure that Cyprus was for them. We had got to know lots of folk in our village and were having a walk round with Ann and Jez when we saw Gary, our builder friend. He said the house near him was for rent and he knew the owner. Also, he had got a key and could show us around. Ann and Jez loved the place and we contacted the owner through Yiannis (the old muktha's assistant or mayor of the village who helped us buy our house) as Gary didn't have a contact number. Then there was a problem. The guy who owned the property had promised it to someone else. This is when we found Yiannis to be useful. He knew the folk that were going to be the new tenants and persuaded Ann and Jez's future landlord to go with them instead.

So now I had another old client who had followed us to Cyprus. We had introduced Ann and Jez to Pat at a barbecue at our house while they were staying with us. Although Ann didn't ride anymore, she still enjoyed the grooming and the looking after bit. Pat had told her she was very welcome to come up to her riding school to groom horses or whatever. That was in September 2012. By Christmas they had sold their UK home and moved to Cyprus full-time.

Very often, Ann liked to come with me on my farrier rounds when I was booked at Pat's. She was a bit apprehensive about riding again due to having a hip replacement and still having a problem with it. That didn't stop her from the looking after bit of the horses. It never bothered her if it was mucking out or grooming or just being the general dogsbody around the stables. Although reluctant to ride because of her hip, she often thought, should she? Pat said if she ever did decide, Mac was the one to try, as he was bombproof. I think Ann must have thought, did she dare, and one day she got on Mac and rode him around the menage for a good 20 minutes. When we were going home, she told me she really enjoyed getting back in the saddle and her dodgy hip hadn't given her any grief.

Ann also went with me to Marlene's at Amargeti. Again, no one asked her to do anything, but it didn't take her long to be grooming this horse and that horse. Mucking out or whatever other jobs needed to be done. When we stopped for coffee Ann told Marlene she really liked some of her horses. Were they bred in Cyprus or had lots had come from other countries? At the time I thought of 40-odd years ago when Ann first helped me to shoe that young difficult horse at Bill's farm. I never imagined that, one day, she would be accompany me on my farrier round in Cyprus and to be living in the same village. As for sitting and having a coffee in Marlene's club house at her riding school up in the hills of Cyprus, I still can't believe it was Ann. I thought she wasn't the type to holiday in a foreign country, never mind living in one.

When we came back to the UK on holiday, we left Ann and Jez with a key and they looked after our house while we were away. I can think of one time we were away in the UK the weather was foul for most of the time. We were with my cousin, Heather, and her husband, Ron, on the sea promenade at Whitby. It was August and the wind and rain was horrendous. Heather took a photo of us on Phyl's phone with us huddled up and getting soaked with what felt like a force eight gale blowing. We emailed the photo over to Ann thinking she would be pitying us for our holiday foul weather. Her reply was, 'You lucky sods. Wish we had it over here. It's absolutely sweltering here.'

She wanted the rain for a different reason to us. It was August and the temperature can hit 40 degrees and the rain would have been a godsend.

DODGY TRADESMEN
AND A FARRIER

In Cyprus I came across lots of folk, and I am embarrassed to say lots were fellow British citizens too, who would give you false information about what their qualified profession or trade was back in the UK. We were caught out by a dodgy builder and nearly one or two who were supposed to be professionals in their line of work.

We had financial consultants ringing us up from time to time, claiming to work for the biggest investment companies in the world. Straightaway that was a warning sign to me because I had never heard of these so-called companies. If I had I would still have taken it with a pinch of salt that they were not actually employed by them and wanted me to invest my money in their own personal bank. If Phyl answered the phone to one of these so-called investment companies she just brushed them off and told them, 'We are skint.'

One, though, I found amusing as soon as he said he was a financial consultant and the first question he asked me was, 'Can I ask you, do you bank onshore or offshore, and over a cup of tea I can call at your home, and at your convenience? I can probably improve your investment and can I be cheeky and ask your age?'

'Can I be cheeky too and ask you do you bank offshore or onshore? Also would it be OK for me to call at your house and over a cup of tea look at your finances and can I be cheeky and ask how old you are too,' I replied bluntly.

'I am 59 years old and have amassed over 40 years of experience in this field of work,' he replied, hoping to have convinced me.

'What, you are still working at 59? I think it would be better for me to come round your house and over a cup of tea let me have a look to see where you have gone wrong with your investments. I could have fully retired at 56 years old. Didn't you invest wisely?' I replied, pleased with my answer and him ending the call abruptly.

I can get very cross when folk ring me out of the blue trying to extract money out of me either by trying to get me to buy something I don't want or those so-called investment scheme consultants. My advice is not to entertain anybody who phones up or knocks on your door without an appointment. I remember one time some firm was trying to sell us something and Phyl answered and said we were not interested. The guy tried his best to convince her and asked if it was best to call back when I was in.

'I think that may be a bad idea if you don't want an earful of abuse,' was her reply, knowing how I hate this cold-calling.

Another guy I caught out big time was an English chap who was passing himself off as a highly trained British farrier. George Hourie had told me about him and he said he was supposed to be an ex-army farrier and who had taught other farriers. When I came across this chap's work, I knew he was never a British trained qualified farrier and I am not certain he was ever a member of the armed forces either. The horses he shod were only shod in front and not very well shod at that. Some of the Cypriot farriers' work was better. If I had done them, I would have been embarrassed with the workmanship and not wanted to have put my name to the job. I know all farriers' work is slightly different, but this chap's work would have caused alarm bells and the Farriers Registration could get involved if he was in the UK.

When I was out on my farrier round one day, I bumped into this so-called brilliant farrier. He tried telling me he had trained lots of Cypriot farriers, including George Hourie, but he had only qualified to fit front shoes when he took his farrier examination in the UK. He said he never got around to sitting the examination for doing the hinds. Well, he must have thought I didn't know the rules and regulations to become a qualified farrier in the UK. There is no examination I know about to allow farriers to fit just the horse's front shoes. We have to qualify to fit hinds too unless I have broken the law for many years fitting shoes on the hind feet as well as the front.

I didn't query him too much about the examinations as I didn't want him to realise he may have been digging himself into a six-foot hole. It was true an ex-army chap did give tuition to George Hourie, but it wasn't him. I personally knew the guy who did teach George who I will call Jim Brown (not his real name) who went on to be a top farrier back in the UK after he left the army. This was when I said, 'I know an ex-army farrier who was out here called Jim Brown. Did you know him? He had told me he had given farrier tuition to one or two farriers when stationed in Cyprus. I had met him just before I moved to Cyprus at a horseshoeing competition on Stoneleigh showground. As for George, he is a big mate of mine. He told me he was lucky to have found a top guy to help him improve his farrier work.'

'You know Jim Brown and George?' he replied nervously.

'Yes, we get to know fellow farriers through the Farriers Association, competitions and other meetings we had in the UK. What's your name?'

'Jim,' came a mumbled reply, without a surname, as that is what folk knew him by but I am sure it was an alias.

I wanted to ask him how he got into shoeing horses in Cyprus but I got the feeling he knew I had sussed him out and I knew he was not a qualified farrier. The more questions I asked about him, the more the answers sounded to me as if he was scraping the bottom of the barrel for the right reply. I think he thought he got himself into a six-foot hole at the beginning of our chat. When he realised I was big friends with George and I knew Jim who had trained him too, he didn't seem to want to talk to me anymore. I thought to myself, he did try to dig himself out of a big hole but now he was now in an 18-foot hole with the cock and bull explanation. Funny thing was, he packed up shoeing horses due to a dodgy back not long afterwards.

We were out with friends when I told them about how I had come across some folk who had moved to Cyprus and would become a professional in whatever work you wanted done. One of our friends told me about this guy I will call Dave, who advertised that his firm had qualified electricians, plumbers, joiners, master builders or whatever tradesman you were looking for. The other thing was that these tradesmen all had 30 to 40 years of experience. What was strange about this firm was there was only one person on the books and his name was Dave. We all thought the same because Dave must be an amazing guy and be over a hundred years old, if not more, if he served his time to qualify for so many trades plus the years of experience. I used to joke I wasn't a farrier in the UK. No, I qualified as a brain surgeon with 40 years' experience.

IF ONLY I WAS 30 YEARS YOUNGER

I often wished I had been 30 years younger from what I know about a farrier life in Cyprus. I hadn't intended to shoe horses ever again when we moved there in 2004. At the time I was 56 years old and although I got asked to trim the donkey's feet at the donkey sanctuary, I never thought I would end up shoeing horses the length and breadth of Cyprus. That including over the border in the Turkish side in the north. Sometimes I felt guilty when I heard some Cypriot people with qualifications were only earning 800 euros a month and I could earn around 500 or more euros a day. I tried to work only two or three days a week but often it got extended to four although some of the extra days I only tried to work in the morning. I thought if I was just starting out, or even in my 30s, I could have had a better life both financially and health-wise. I didn't have to contend with as much bad weather and muddy hooves. Although the temperatures could be in the high 30s in summer, I did what the Cypriots do and that is get up early and be at the first horse as soon as the sun was rising. I wanted to be finished by lunchtime in the summer months when it did get too hot. I never had had a problem to get up in the morning even in the UK as

I often got to my first call before six o'clock in the morning or earlier in the summer months. In fact, I love to be out at the crack of dawn when the air feels fresher. Also, I always think your day goes much better from an early start and you can get through more work in the morning than the afternoon. Mind you, in Cyprus I always did look for shade to work under, either a stable or a tree, even in winter.

Then again, I can remember it being in the middle of January and the temperatures still in the mid-20s. I thought how nice it was to be working outside in the sun and not in the cold damp British weather. I thought about the dark winter days back in the UK when the daylight often got bad around two o'clock in the afternoon and the temperature dropped rapidly to minus-blooming-Moscow. Then, to make matters even more trying, it started to rain or snow and did its best to disrupt my day. I think of the times when the horse owner would get their horse into a stable or barn to be out of the winter elements and say they could switch the light on. Often this light consisted of one 40-watt bulb that glimmered a flickering light no more than a candle from the rafters. With your head down trying to shoe horses, it was more or less is like shoeing blind and, boy, did the job seem to take forever to finish.

Although we did get one or two dodgy days when the weather was unsettled it wasn't many and it never lasted very long. I sometimes smile when I hear folk moan in the UK when the sun does come out and the thermometer goes into the high 20s and it's too hot to work. I found that my body adapted to cope with the heat and the high 20s I didn't mind. It was better than the freezing cold winter days in the UK.

Mind you, I did think I was mad once or twice when it got into the 40s while shoeing horses in northern Cyprus in the height of summer. When I had to get a hot horseshoe out my mobile gas forge it felt like 10,000 degrees of heat had hit me. You could say it made me perspire a little. I lie there – my clothes were wet through with sweat and stuck to my body. That was when I found it was a bad idea to wear a t-shirt instead of one that is fastened with buttons at the front. At Di's stables in the north, I always had a wash and changed my clothes before I left for the journey home. It felt ten degrees hotter than the south of the island. The biggest job was to get my wet sweaty t-shirt off. The blooming thing was stuck to me. I thought I may need John's help. I did eventually manage to get it off by rolling it up bit by bit. Once I had managed to free one of my arms it was a big relief to get it over my head. I didn't want the others to have a good laugh at my expense. I did manage it on my own eventually in the end but it must have taken me a good five minutes. I had visions of getting stuck with one arm half out. I am sure the grooms and John would have had a good laugh at my mishap if I had.

MY BODY IS TELLING
ME TO SLOW DOWN

Yes, I loved the hustle and bustle of the life at stable yards in Cyprus. Although I shod horses until I was 68 years old, I found over the last two years I was starting to struggle. One problem was I was not as strong as I used to be and as I had mentioned in my first book, psoriasis had been a pain to me since I was 25 years old. Although it had never bothered me too much since we lived in Cyprus, it suddenly decided to erupt when Phyl and I came back to the UK for a month's holiday in August 2014. The day we were due to fly I didn't actually feel ill but I felt very lethargic. Jez, our friend, had offered to run us to the airport for our 8pm flight. Jez was a guy who hated to be late so we thought he would be picking us up around 5:30pm to be at the airport for 6pm. Two hours before departure at 8pm. That night I could have got into bed instead of an aircraft. I just didn't understand what could be wrong with me to feel the way I did.

Jez came at 5pm. He was very early but, never mind, we were ready, so we left for Paphos airport. At the check-in we were told there was an hour's delay for our flight to Manchester. This felt a major issue to me. I know this often happens and usually I would just accept it but I found myself feeling uneasy for no reason and probably muttered something under my breath. With the hustle and bustle of the airport, I felt overwhelmed. Although on the outside I didn't show it, my stomach was doing cartwheels. I had never had this feeling before. In the departure lounge I couldn't seem to get comfortable on the seats. A young couple with their very young children were trying their best to calm their crying kids. Usually things like babies crying or tired toddlers screaming doesn't bother me. I may even have volunteer to help. That night they seemed to scream for hours although it was only five minutes and not piercing tantrums.

The flight ended up leaving nearly two hours later instead of the hour delay and I couldn't seem to get comfortable in the aircraft seat. To top it off for a bad night we were flying into a strong headwind which meant arrival time was later. That flight felt it took five days instead of five hours. The only thing that went right that night was our cases were the first to arrive on the baggage carrousel.

On leaving the airport terminal we made our way to the bus stop, for the bus, which would take us to the car hire building. At our stop bollards had been placed around the bus stop shelter as if it was out of bounds. So we waited like others did at the side. Buses kept coming and going but none that would take us to the car rental department. We waited and waited and even asked one of the other bus drivers if buses for the car rental department ran all night and they told us they did. We had booked an overnight stay in an airport hotel before we travelled to a cottage we had rented in North Yorkshire. By now it had gone past three o'clock in the morning and all I wanted, desperately, was some sleep. My head was telling me it was gone 5 o'clock Cypriot-time. Eventually the bus did come after a guy who collected up luggage trolleys asked if we had ordered the bus.

'Order the bus? I didn't know we had to. Where do I do that?' I asked, thinking it was something we should have done online when we booked the car.

'Pick up the phone in the shelter,' he replied.

'It's petitioned off. I thought it was out of bounds,' I muttered.

'No take no notice of that. Just pick the phone up and say that you want a bus to the car hire.'

We must have waited God knows how long and all we had to do was go round the blooming bollards to order a bus which only took a few minutes to arrive. We couldn't understand why it was blocked off in the first place. It didn't look as if there was an issue or work in progress. When we finally arrived at the car hire, I just happened to say to the guy at the reception about the hotel we were hoping to stay at for what was left of the night. We told him we had booked airport accommodation, and I said, 'The directions online for our hotel recommended we go to the motorway, go down one junction that leads back onto the airport. We would see our hotel is on the left.'

I had just checked with the car hire chap that was the best way, thinking he would say, *that's right, it is the easiest route*, but he didn't.

He said, 'No stay on the airport and take this turn then that turn go over this roundabout and that roundabout and take the third turn on the last one. Your hotel is on the left.'

Well that seemed straightforward but I was half-asleep and even though it was the middle of the night, the airport traffic was still very busy. After taking a few left- then right-turns we saw a roundabout straight over like the guy told us. The next one. Was it this one where we take the third turn or the next, I thought! Well that was the wrong roundabout to take the third turn. As soon as I saw the slip road that led back onto the motorway, I realised it was the wrong roundabout. If I had followed the route the hotel had advised, we should have been leaving the motorway instead of joining it at this junction. It should have been the next roundabout where I took the third turn. With cars behind me, I was committed and had no choice but to join the motorway and we were now on the way to North Wales instead of Yorkshire. It seemed miles before the next junction where we were able to come back. On the way back we could see our hotel from the motorway but the slip road on the side going east was blocked off for road works. By now it was a quarter to five in the morning and I looked at Phyl and I think she thought the same as me and said, 'Sod it, let's forget the hotel and head for the holiday cottage at Appleton-le-Moors in North Yorkshire.' I had known the cottage owners, Lyn and Barry, for over 60-odd years as I had started primary school with Barry.

On the first day when we were settled into the cottage, I noticed my skin bubbling up as if psoriasis was on the verge of irrupting and it was feeling very uncomfortable. Next morning I was covered head to toe with flaking skin. I must have emptied the local chemist shop of any greasy ointment that would ease my sore skin on that holiday. Over the years I have suffered with psoriasis, I have found lotions or potions just helped for half an hour for relief when the psoriasis was as bad I got it. The way I can describe it is when covered head to toe is like being dressed in sandpaper. We were away for a month and the psoriasis showed no sign of easing up and by the end of the holiday I felt like the singing detective from the '80s television series. I had horses booked when our holiday ended and I wasn't looking forward to working with how my sore skin felt.

At Pat's riding school I did her horses in two sittings. One batch would take me three quarters of a day and the others just a morning if that. I was glad this booking was only three full sets but instead of it taking a morning it took me all day. I was nipping into her little cloakroom two or three times per horse to rub greasy ointment into my scaly skin to give relief for half an hour. I thought, *I can't carry on like this*, but was pleased I managed to get Pat's horses shod.

The next day, a Friday morning, and in a desperate state, I walked into Paphos hospital. I paid 15 euros at reception and asked if I could see a dermatologist. I was told to wait round the corner on the left.

After only a 15-to-20-minute wait it was my turn. I knew I could have one more shot at P.U.V.A light treatment that had worked for me in the UK. The reason I say one more shot is because it is radiation treatment and only so many sessions are allowed. When the dermatologist examined me, he agreed to start the treatment the following Tuesday but first I had to have a blood test and a chest X-ray. An hour and half later I walked out of that hospital with the results of my blood test and the chest X-ray results in my hand.

Two weeks later, the psoriasis had subsided and I felt more comfortable after the P.U.V.A treatment (P.U.V.A is the acronym for Psoralen+ultraviolet light A).

I was 67 years old at the time and I decided I was going to cut down on my work still further. I had told other folk, 'IT'S NO GOOD BEING THE RICHEST PERSON IN THE GRAVEYARD,' when they had health problems. I thought it was time I told myself the same thing. Also, I felt I was not as strong as I used to be. I had started to dread the prospect of shoeing some horses. I don't mean the plain bad-tempered ones, but the ones that probably lent on me or fidgeted a little while I shod them. I would probably never have noticed when I was fitter that they were leaning on me or whatever. Now any little movement or lean I was finding it difficult, strength-wise, to cope. I am not blaming the horse or the owner, it was my body trying to tell me I was not as strong as I used to be. I felt what would have been easy for a younger person who would never have noticed a horse leaning on them, became a little harder work for me.

A year before I had given up traveling to places like Limassol and into the north of Cyprus. A young English farrier called Martin had come to see me to say he was moving to Cyprus. At the time I told him I could pass work on to him and seeing as he was going to be living nearer to Limassol I would pass the stables on to him that were a far distance away for me but nearer for him. After this last eruption of psoriasis, I knew I needed to cut my workload down just to two or three horses a week and passed a lot more work on to Martin.

I still went to Pat's and two or three other yards for another year or so but although these horses were well behaved it felt to me I was psyching myself up to go to work. I started to get an overwhelmed feeling if I had got just one horse to shoe as if it was too much work. I know when I was in my prime in the UK, I thought the other way if I had booked too many horses in. I had the strength and stamina to work until I finished at God knows what time in the evening. Now I wondered if I got the strength to shoe one horse by lunch time. I don't know if it was the latest eruption of psoriasis that had took its toll on me or what but before the last bout I enjoyed shoeing horses. Now it had come a bind for me.

In my first book I mentioned about the time I had met an old farrier at a stable yard in the UK. I was 23 years old at the time and boasting how many horses I had shod that day. It was late one afternoon and Albert, an old farrier I knew, was packing up for the day. He was pleased with himself as he had shod six horses that day (50 years ago, farriers made all their own horseshoes from scratch unlike the variety of ready-mades on the market today. So to make six sets of shoes and to go out and fit was a good day's work). Me, being a cocky 23-year-old said, 'Six? I can get that amount done by breakfast,' trying to show off even though I hadn't.

It must have been 5 o'clock in the afternoon when Albert was packing up and I had arrived to start to shoe three horses all round and with bags of energy. Albert then asked how old I was as he was nearly 60 years old and I have never forgotten what he said: 'How old are you, Mick?'

'I'm 23,' I replied, trying to indicate shoeing six horses a day was like half a day's work to me.

'Well, Mick, I am nearly 60. When I was 23, I had lots of energy like you. When I hit 40 I realised I had slowed down a bit. At 50 my energy had declined a bit more and I am nearly 60. You are saying six horses is like half a day's work to you. Well, I feel proud I have managed this amount,' replied Albert.

I have never forgotten Albert's words and by golly was he right. I did have bags of energy, and I suppose I was trying to be a show off but I realised later in life show-offs can get caught out. Albert's lecture to me certainly become true. I too found myself not as quick at 40. In my 50s it had started to take me a little longer still to shoe a horse and I admired Albert still being fit enough to make six sets and fit them in a day. I did keep shoeing horses beyond retirement age and yes, I also have shod six in a day but I cheated, I had used machine-made horseshoes. I did make my own horseshoes from scratch years ago but with an improved variety of readymade horseshoes on the market, it cut out the time spent making them. I can remember, years ago, it became a routine to spend evenings in my forge making horseshoes for an early start the following morning.

The last couple of years I did find it hard work. I had cut my work load down to just a very few clients but never mind shoeing six a day, one now had become a trial. Now I was worrying how I was going to manage one or even two horses. It was not that the horses were difficult to shoe or dodgy owners. No, the owners and horses were a pleasure to have as clients. I thought when I did start shoeing horses in Cyprus, I would be still doing it until the time came to put me in a wooden box. I have heard other farriers say the same thing that once they got to retirement age that they would still be shoeing horses until the day that they died. Then two or three years later they realise their body was worn out. With me, although I enjoyed the hustle and bustle of stable yards and I still do, it was not the actual shoeing of the horses I started to dread. It was the physical bit my body couldn't cope with. I tried to reason why I felt like this. After all, if I had only had one or two horses to shoe when I was in the UK, I would be thinking that would be a very slack day.

THE GOOD TIMES WE HAD

Phyl and I had lived in Cyprus for 11 and a half years and both of us had enjoyed our time living in a very old Cypriot village. We had got used to their way of life and had many Cypriot friends too. Phyl had joined various art groups and managed to sell several of her paintings at exhibitions. Also, when some businesses found out she was an accountant, she had got asked to do their books. Not to mention the brilliant social life we had. We often attended this function and that function and the endless friends we had met both English and Cypriot and of course Valentine from Bulgaria.

Would we miss having a meal in some village in an old Cypriot village tucked away up in the hills? Of course we would! I can still hear the laughter of the locals chatting in a fast loud voice which they spoke in when excited. Another thing I learned was not to scoff a meze down in record time. The Cypriots would still be eating two or three hours after being served the first potions of the meze. I can remember the time we were with friends, Margaret and Bob, and we had ordered one of the best mezes I ever had had. The restaurant is in a village called Kallepia in the hills not far from Paphos and was run by a father and his daughter. The father was lovely chap and was the head man at the police station in Paphos. Their hospitality and food were superb. The first few dishes of the meze were so delicious that we scoffed the lot. Well, this meant we hadn't had enough and we got more of the same dish and we ate that too. After eating double helpings of three or four potions of this meze, it started to take an effect. When the staff were bringing the next potion out and with several more to go at, we had to ask them to stop as we were stuffed. That was when we realised our mistake. No matter how tasty the food is, it is better to leave a little and take your time. What looks like small potions to begin with would be a very big plateful if all the different dishes were put on your plate in one go.

Three weeks later, when we were in Kallepia with Bob and Margaret again, we went for another meze. This time we asked if we could start the meze where we stopped at on our previous visit. We were only joking and the father, who I will call Petros, knew we were only joking too. This time he said, 'siga, siga' (meaning slowly, slowly), with a big grin on his face.

Over the years we had numerous meals at Kallepia. Petros treated his customers very generously and also had a wicked sense of humour. After the diners were near to the end of their meal, Petros liked to give his customers a drink on the house before leaving for home. This night cap was zivania, which was distilled in some makeshift distillery somewhere up in the hills. Yes, this stuff was rocket fuel and not recommended if you were driving. The same stuff the old lady with the lame donkey had given to me a few years before. Sure enough, he offered some to me and I said, 'Depends who the policeman is tonight, Petros!'

'I can give you a note to say you are my friend if the police stop you,' he replied laughing.

I don't know if he meant what he said but I didn't want to chance it. The limit for driving with alcohol is lower in Cyprus than the UK. Mind you, lots of the locals never get prosecuted because they may be a cousin to someone in the police force. Another reason I refused this rocket fuel was it was near Christmas and Paphos police get moved to Nicosia, Limassol and Larnaca and so forth. The reason was drunken drivers may not have a relation in another town's police department. So I figured even if Petros had given me a note it may have got disregarded if I was stopped.

The times I had heard siga siga, meaning slowly slowly, was beginning to make sense to me and I heard myself saying it to friends that were visiting from the UK. Mind you, if you were dining out in the busy tourist resorts the mezes and other meals on offer were nowhere as nice or cooked to the same standard as the village tavernas tucked away up in the hills. The tourist restaurants want the diners in and out for a quick turnaround. I did find something useful to do if you were dining out in one of these tourist establishments was to let the staff know that you lived full-time in Cyprus. We used to say something like, 'God it's hot down here compared to Koili where we live.' That meant a 10% discount off the bill if they thought you were a local.

We were with Charles and Barbara, who owned their own restaurant where Phyl helped out. We had gone for a meal at a venue that put on entertainment more for people on holiday. It was on the one day of the week that Charles and Barbara had off. We had ordered a bottle of red wine (I can't remember what brand). It was at a price, although not cheap, that we could all afford.

The waiter had hardly had time to leave our table when the manager appeared to tell us the wine we had ordered was out of stock. He apologised but he could recommend something similar. The waiter brought this "similar wine" and he made a fuss of splashing and swirling it around the glass for Charles to taste. Charles said it tasted exactly like the one out of stock and it would be fine. We were then entertained by the wine poured into a decanter and swirled around as if it was washing the glass sides. Then each of our glasses had to be cleaned with a tea towel before the waiter could fill our glasses. Then with the tea towel draped over his arm, he put on another show. It was as if he was trying to show he had a university degree in how to pour wine into a glass.

We found the meal OK but we all agreed it was nothing special. We sat chatting and decided to order another bottle of this "similar wine". Again we got the same show of the bottle emptied into a decanter and swished around, hoping we would be impressed by their professional approach. Well, their professional approach didn't impress us when we got the bill. This "similar wine" was more than twice the price of the one we had originally ordered. When we queried it with the manager he said, 'It's similar in taste, not the price.' We thought they had done this on purpose thinking we were on holiday and they would never to see us again.

When Charles said, 'I have a restaurant at Chlorakas and would never dream offering my clients something more than twice the price without telling them,' we saw a different look on this chap's face when he realised we lived on the island and we could badmouth him to everyone we met. This manager changed his tune and tried to apologise. He must have said sorry God knows how many times and decided to give us a "special price". I thought about it later as none of us saw the label on the bottle the wine came out of. It was quickly tipped into a decanter and the empty bottle was taken away by another waiter. Charles, who did know his wines, said it tasted exactly the same. I often wondered if it was what we had ordered in the first place and "similar in taste" was their way of an excuse to charge more. That was another good reason to hint you are a full-time resident even if you weren't.

Our social life is what I will cherish when we moved to Koili. We were living in the real Cyprus where no one was in rush and tear mode. Farmers would travel at a snail's pace on what looked to me like a rotavator engine adapted to pull a trailer with a seat at the front of the trailer for the driver. A bit like Tom and Barbara Good in the television program, *The Good Life*. I also got asked to trim one or two of the villagers' donkeys. If they were short of money to pay me, they were perhaps too generous with produce. The times I had come home with big potions of halloumi cheese, vegetables and other delicious Cypriot delicacies superbly cooked.

I remember Luka and Socrates who we became big friends with. I had got to know Luka when his donkey was in desperate need of a farrier. They often joined Phyl and myself for a chat at Lagis's local coffee shop. I say coffee shop as Lagis and his other half did meals. They offered a very tasty meze plus other Cypriot cuisine, and it wasn't just coffee they sold for a liquid refreshment. I had a beer and Phyl had a red wine when we had had our meal one evening when Luka and Socrates joined us. In Cyprus, especially in the villages, beer is served with a small glass where you have got to keep topping it up, and it was through Luka and Socrates I found out why. I first thought they were cheeky devils topping their glasses up with my beer. Once the bottle was empty, one of them would go and buy another bottle then top my glass up from it. Then the other one would replace that next empty bottle. The idea is your beer stays cooler if you are with others and share. That is why beer didn't come with a pint glass.

The Cypriot village taverna and coffee shops were never in a rush and the locals made us feel welcome when we moved there. The village was not big but we had the choice of three coffee shops plus a tavern and a corner shop. Our house was in the middle of all of them.

At another one run by Costa and his wife (not the worldwide outlet brand) we had never paid for a drink and it wasn't for the want of trying. A lovely old guy called Neofytos would often tell us to join him for a coffee and a chat if we were walking past. He would be sitting at one of the outdoor tables and would insist we join him and he would pay for our coffee. We knew most of the village folk were connected one way or another with goat rearing and farming, but Neofytos was a chef. He had lived in the UK with his English wife and since losing her to cancer he had moved back to Cyprus. We could tell in his voice that he really missed her. He was an interesting guy who loved to chat about anything but was sick of hearing how bad rearing goats and farming was from folk connected to farming.

They were always moaning how little money was made from farming.

Neofytos lived with his dog which he adored, although he did have a daughter who did visit him from time to time. One Sunday we never expected to have Costa waiting for us at our garden gate when we returned from walking our dog, Jack (our Bearded Collie.) Costa was in a panic and a crowd had congregated outside the coffee shop and Neofytos's house on the opposite side of the road. Neofytos's dog was barking and they thought he was in need of help but daren't go in case the dog would attack. They had even called the police but lots of Cypriots are weary of strange dogs. I quickly put Jack in our house while Phyl ran to assist to get Neofytos's dog. When I got there, she had found the back door unlocked and had her arms around the dog's neck. It was waging its tail and looked relieved that help had arrived. I arrived a minute later and used Jack's lead. By the look on some of the local's faces, they thought the dog was barking in an aggressive manner. We knew that dog hadn't got a vicious streak. We had met it loads of times and it loved any fuss that we were prepared to give. I think why the poor thing was barking was to attract attention that our friend Neofytos had passed away without any warning. Mind you, I felt we were like a hero for capturing a vicious dog.

JAMES AND LISA

It was something I could get used to, a comment my old mate Andy Speck's youngest son James said. He was also a farrier like his brother, Richard, following their father's footsteps. He was on his honeymoon with his new wife, Lisa, to Cyprus when James made the remark. They came to see us and we treated him to a meal at the Last Castle as a wedding present. This restaurant is off the beaten track in the Akamas which is an unspoilt rugged area next to the sea. It is far away from the hustle and bustle life of the folk on holiday. The Last Castle is on top of a hill and from a distance looks no more than a shack. The stone tables are under a big grapevine that nearly covers the entire eating area and resembles something out of the Stone Age. I think Fred Flintstone may have got involved in designing the place but the setting is perfect. All the diners got an unobstructed view of the valley below and beyond. I could tell that James and Lisa loved the food too. There is no menu. You could have either two potions of pork or two chicken, or one of each, cooked over a spit. The taste was to die for with no gristle or fat in the pork. Salad with dressing and massive roasted chips, with lovely fresh bread. We had to book every time we went as the place was always busy. James told me it was the best meal he had in Cyprus and loved the setting where we had taken them to and could get used to our life in Cyprus too.

A couple of years later his dad, Andy, and mum, Jacky, visited us and we took them there too. I can remember Andy commenting on his meal at the Last Castle as he never knew chicken could taste like it did. I had no idea what herbs or spices were used for the flavouring, but whatever ingredients were added, it certainly worked. The Specks were not the only ones we introduced to the Last Castle.

John and Jane, some of our friends, had never dined there before, although they lived in Cyprus. It was the end of the season and it was nearly on the last day before they closed for the winter. That day we had just got served with our food when a slight drizzle of rain started to descend on us. Not where we would get soaking wet as the grape vine tree above did give us a bit of shelter. I can remember John taking a few bites of his pork and said, 'I don't care how hard it rains, I am not shifting until I have finished.' Although the rain never came to anything, I am sure he would have meant what he said as a bit of rain was in no way going to stop him enjoying his meal. I think we would have all agreed with him.

This laid-back way of living felt a million miles from the rat race I had become accustomed to before moving to Cyprus. I enjoyed spending many hours with friends in a relaxed atmosphere and dining outdoors under the stars on a lovely warm moonlit evening. Well, that was paradise for me and that was something I didn't have to psych myself up to do.

PHYL'S BOOKKEEPING
AND ACCOUNTS

One business got Phyl to do their books and we felt something wasn't right from the start. The owners, a husband and wife, ran a café in a busy tourist spot in Kato Paphos. Every time we passed it or went in to return their books at the end of the month it always looked to be quite busy. What Phyl had got given in receipts and sales showed they were spending more than they were taking. This didn't seem to bother them when Phyl queried it with them. That was until they wanted to sell the business. They wanted Phyl to create a false set of books.

An accountant can only do accounts for what information they receive off a business. If they produce false accounts for tax reasons or other purposes, it is fraud. As soon as they said they wanted her to do a second set to sell their café business, we told them to find someone else. We knew they were on the fiddle to make it look as if they were losing money instead of making it for tax purposes. She couldn't prove it, but we had a good idea that was the reason. If Phyl had created another set of books that would have proved she knew there was some fiddling going on. The trouble was, if she had created a new set of books it may have been nearer to what they should have been declaring.

When she told me, we both thought it best to take their dodgy documents back to them and say we were not interested to even think about doing something which was fraud. The last thing we would have wanted would be for Phyl to be hauled before a foreign court. That was left for me as we thought if Phyl took that month's uncompleted books back, they might have tried to convince her to do it for them. Sure enough, they did try it with me but were not happy when I refused. They tried to tell me it was important that the books were up to date that week. Well, that was their problem as far as we were concerned.

Another person she helped out was Simon who sold cars. We even bought a five-year-old Rav4 off him which we ran for eight years. That car never gave us one bit of trouble in all the years we owned it although it was showing its age when we swapped it for a two-year-old Suzuki Swift in 2015. Simon asked Phyl would she mind doing his paper work at his car showroom and attend to the odd customer if he was out. Mind you, no one could have missed her sitting at her desk, next to the showroom window, in a bright orange t-shirt with Simon's name on to advertise his car showroom. Also, she would come home and tell me Simon got her to deliver or collect some very expensive cars or whatever. Although he had employed her only a couple of mornings a week, he treated her well.

We had bought our old Rav4 off him which never gave us one bit of trouble apart from developing a knocking sound on the front suspension not long after we bought it. Simon got various mechanics to inspect it but no one could find a problem. Simon asked Ian, who wasn't a mechanic but did odd jobs around the showroom, to take our car to a place up the road that specialised in car suspension and they couldn't find anything amiss either. Ian reported to Simon on his return that the knocking sound sounded terrible. Straightaway he got down on his hands and knees and inspected where this knocking could be coming from. It didn't take him long to see the problem and went and got a socket set. Phyl said she watched him and he sorted it in a few minutes. A nut had worked loose and was about to fall off. Ian said to Simon it wasn't very lose then, after watching him tighten the nut up with several turns of his wrench.

When our car was ready for its yearly service, Simon wouldn't let us pay for it. Although he didn't own the garage that repaired or serviced his cars, he would arrange for ours to be serviced while she was on duty at the showroom. Although a year or so later, he did buy that business too. Then, at Christmas, he would treat all his staff including partners to a festive meal. We used to think he was too generous.

When I started to shoe horses, Simon found me a five-year-old Ford Connect van. It too served me well for several years and if the truth was known it may have been overloaded with all my farrier kit it had to carry. It never complained and although it went down many unmade roads and rough tracks it seemed to manage them with ease.

JORDAN

I was not sure if I would ever be ready to leave Cyprus and the many people, Cypriot, British and other nationalities, we had made friends with. Our lifestyle felt like paradise to me. I thought of the countries like Jordan we went on holiday to. Places I would have never dreamt of visiting. Jordan was only a 90-minute flight from Cyprus. We had booked the trip to include a car and driver to take us from the airport in Amman to Petra, have a few days there before moving to a hotel at the Dead Sea (the Dead Sea, air, and salt is good for psoriasis).

On arriving in Jordan, our travel agent told us we would be met at the airport and they would sort our tourist visas that were required. Sure enough, as soon as we entered the airport building, we saw a chap holding a placard with our name. The first thing he asked was, 'Do you have a visa or do we have to get one?'

'Our travel agent told us we can get one at the airport,' I replied, hoping the travel agent had told us right.

'No problem, follow me,' he said as he pushed to the front of a long queue of folk waiting for their turn to be issued with a visa.

We hesitated as we were not sure if we had to wait for our turn but this chap said, 'Come, come,' and waved his arm, instructing us to follow him. I felt as if I ought to apologise to the people waiting patiently for jumping the long queue. We gave our names and address and whatever other details the staff wanted to know. Then we had to go to another counter to have our photograph taken. Again, another long queue and this guy just pushed to the front waving his arm for us to follow him and I felt as if I should be saying sorry to the folk for us jumping this second queue.

I think it must have taken him less than ten minutes to sort our visas. This was done before our luggage had arrived on the carrousel. He then told us our driver was waiting and in no time we were on the way to Petra. I hate to think how long it would have taken without this guy's help.

At Petra, we wanted to see the temple carved out of the rocks in the year 312BC. It was the setting for one of the *Indiana Jones* films. We were advised by the travel company it was best to book a horse ride, at a small fee, to ride down to this monumental structure as it is over very rough terrain. It probably is the route the horse took but folk do walk down on a more even pathway. We were also advised to have a guide who we found to be a must. The Petra entrance is between the narrow walkway between the rock walls. This is why you need a guide who shows and explains little gulley's carved into the rocks for collecting rain water and drainage and so forth. The things he pointed out I would never have noticed if we were on our own. Then when you see the temple carved into the rock face, it can take your breath away how men with limited tools could create such a work of art.

Getting back to the horse ride, I was riding behind Phyl's horse and instead of admiring the scenery, my farrier mode kicked in. I couldn't help notice her horse's hind shoes. I know some farriers like to shoe with plenty of length but this looked ridiculous. The shoe must have stuck out at the back of the heels by three or four inches. I thought perhaps it was to help it to ski down the sandy hills. When we arrived at the beginning of the Petra entrance, we had to dismount and meet our guide. My first job, though, was to inspect this horse's hind shoes.

I couldn't believe what I saw. It looked like someone had tried to nail shoes on where they touched. I think the guy who fitted the horse's shoes thought as long as the horse went clip-clop afterwards that was all that mattered. Those shoes I was certain were not made for that horse. To me it looked like some guy had got two shoes he had found and nailed them on regardless, even though they were miles too big. The guide saw me looking unimpressed and asked me if I worked with horses. I told him I was a British farrier and I said, 'These shoes look to be miles too big or is there a reason for the heels to be stuck out like they were?'

The guide was not impressed either and said, 'If you inspected the whole 300 horses back at the stables you would have a fit at the workmanship. The guys that shoe horses are not properly trained and most have not got a clue what they are doing. If the shoes fit where they happen to touch the hoof that is good enough.'

Then he spoke to another guide and they asked me if I would be interested to come to Jordan to shoe them and give some tuition. He told me there is no regulations in Jordan for farriers, unlike the UK. It is a bit hit and miss if the horse walks away sound after being shod and it is often through pure luck. Some of the horseshoeing here made the Cypriot farriers look brilliant. I thought if only I was 30 years younger I would have enjoyed that challenge. It did cross my mind to ring one or two farrier friends to see if they would give me a hand, as these two guys did mean what they said.

Mind you, I have said many times when I am on holiday, I will not broadcast that I am a farrier. On one holiday years ago in the UK, I ended up shoeing a horse at an attraction about how folk worked in days gone by. They had got folk working on spinning Jennies and other crafts that were slowly dying out. I had heard the sound of hammering at an anvil. I had to be nosy and saw two guys trying to make some gate hinges. I could see they were not properly trained blacksmiths. They were trying their best to put a show on. When I told them I had a forge but I made horseshoes one of the guys told me they needed me. I thought they were going to ask me to give them some tuition on how to make gate hinges. No, he went off and found the owner of a carthorse that gave rides to the museum customers. The guy who owned the horse asked, 'Can you refit the old horse's shoes? The shoes are not worn out but it is badly in need of a foot trim and the shoes refitting.'

'I have no kit with me. I am on holiday,' I muttered.

'We have,' replied the museum owner, not letting me have an excuse.

I looked at my wife as I often said I wouldn't look at horses while on holiday and heard myself saying, 'OK, can I do it tomorrow when I have changed into the worst of my knocking about attire?'

The next day I became one of the attractions with a horseshoeing display. The kit I got supplied with had some very ancient tools. Some had had their day and were only meant for display. The old rasp they supplied wouldn't have been much use to grate cheese never mind to level a horse's hoof. Somehow, I did manage to get the horse shod and was paid more or less double what I had asked for. The times I have said I will not look at horses while on holiday still goes on to this present day. Have I stopped, no, because my mouth often opens before my brain engages to tell me to keep it shut!

SANDY'S FRIEND

Phyl had got to know a lady called Sandy (not the lady who owned the horse) who restored antique furniture. She had advised us that an old wardrobe that had been left in our house which we were going to chop up for firewood was worth at least 1000 Cyprus pounds. All it needed was 5O quid spending on it to bring it back to its former glory. We had our doubts as the builders who renovated our house had put it in the garden thinking the same as us – that it was only fit for firewood. Sandy persuaded us not to burn it and to let her have a go at making it look like a nice piece of antique furniture. The trouble was it was so heavy that it took three of us to lift it onto the double cab truck I had at the time. By this time the wardrobe had stood in the garden for around three months in weather which was sometimes torrential rain but with piercing heat from the sun too.

Two months later, Sandy had worked on the wardrobe around her other work as she knew we were not desperate for it. When she told us it was ready for collection, we couldn't believe our eyes as it didn't look like the wreck of the wardrobe that I had left her with. We did use it for several years before we rearranged our bedroom when we had no use for it.

We told Sandy we were thinking of selling and she said she had contacts with a man who dealt with old furniture. I had an idea we wouldn't get anywhere near the 1000 Cyprus pounds Sandy had thought it could be worth. The currency had now changed to euros due to Cyprus joining the European Union and with a bit of haggling we got €700. I thought not a bad profit for something that was going to be chopped up for firewood.

Over the years, Sandy did lots of work for us and fixed a broken Parker Knowles chair. This chair had sentimental value to me as I had bought a pair of them in 1970 plus a table for five shillings (25p) at an auction. The chairs have remained in my life and even though they were cheap they were the start of my family life.

One chair got broken, though, when a couple who weighed 25 stone-plus each were in our holiday let. The chairs were part of the furniture in the guest annex on our house which we rented out to folk on holiday. The first day this couple arrived, the man came to me with the string that you pull to switch the fan on that is attached to the ceiling light in the bedroom. Instead of giving it a light tug to switch the fan on, they had given it a right old yank and pulled the cable out of the switch. He didn't apologise as a new switch was needed but laughed and said, 'I have got a job for you. Can you fix this tonight?' It was at 8 o'clock on a Saturday night and I needed a new part and everywhere was shut so I couldn't do anything about it. Luckily the fan was on and the light off. They just had to switch it on and off at the light switch on the wall and they would have to use the bedside lights for light instead of the ceiling light.

I fixed the switch in the ceiling light when the shops opened on the Monday morning. I got that job done and a couple of days later they told me they had broken one of the Parker Knowles chairs. Again, no apology but they thought it was funny how it happened. The wife said she was playing a computer game that was plugged into the television and was perched on the front of the chair instead seated right in it. She had got excited that she was winning or whatever and started to bounce her 25-stone-plus weight up and down on the edge of the seat and broke the dowel rods that held the chair together.

When Sandy saw what was broken, she thought it would be the ones at the back of the chair where all the person's weight would be, and not the front. Also the broken dowels showed no sign that they had needed attention. It was just the woman's obese body and jumping up and down that had caused the damage. Sandy did fix it to be like new again though.

Another thing we had noticed was that they used the upright chairs that were around the outside dining table and never the sunbeds when outdoors. We had several metal beds for sunbathing and I realised why they didn't use them apart from the first few days of their holiday. When they left, I found the framework on the whole lot bent and the covering ripped. This couple were just too heavy for them. Mind you, I could understand why both of them were so fat when I found out they used to go to this little village restaurant for breakfast every morning. We were told they both ate two full English breakfasts each every morning they were on holiday. I know where they went and most average folk would be stuffed after one. Also, they had bragged to me how they had to upgrade on British Airways as they were too big to fit in the economy class seats. I don't know how they would have managed on the budget airlines that don't have that facility.

Phyl had got to know Sandy when she helped Charles and Barbara at the restaurant. She was a lady who could have you rolling around laughing if she was telling a story about something that had happened to her in her life. On occasions we both would meet her at different functions that we attended. Although Sandy was more Phyl's friend and often phoned Phyl and if I answered I would shout for Phyl. One night she said, 'It's you I want, Mick. A Cypriot friend's best race horse is a bit lame and I wondered if you had any ideas why.'

'In what way is it lame?' I asked.

'I don't know as I don't know anything about horses,' replied Sandy.

'Where is the horse? Is it local, Sandy?'

'Omodos near to the donkey sanctuary at Vouni. Do you still go there? My friend is called Andros and would appreciate some advice.'

I was still trimming the donkeys' hooves at the donkey sanctuary at the time and arranged to meet Andros at his stables a day or so later after I had seen to the donkeys. John was with me and we couldn't believe our eyes when we first saw this lame horse. One of the hind legs was the size of a tree trunk. Wherever you pressed, pus squirted out by the bucketful from the top of its leg right down to the hoof. I found he had used the same lady vet for two months and she had prescribed antibiotics by the lorry load on every visit and there was not a sign of it getting better. I thought that it needed to be drained somehow and we got hold of Yiannis, hoping that he could help. I thought we would have to insert tubes into several places on the animal's leg and work from that. I did help Yiannis and after a month the horse's hind led started to shrink to more of a normal size. Four months later there was no sign of any lameness and the horse was back in training and shod.

Mind you, I did laugh at Andros when Yiannis asked him if the horse would be retired if it couldn't race anymore. We both thought he would either use it as a brood mare or something just to hack out on now and then. He replied, jokingly, 'Yiannis, if you can't cure the problem, and the horse is no good for racing, you see that cliff edge, it will go over that and you with it. So do your best.' The horse did recover and was even fit enough for the racetrack.

Yes, Andros had my sense of humour and was also very generous. On that first day when he asked for my opinion, I got the feeling he trusted me. Although that first day I couldn't do a lot without Yiannis's help! Andros insisted that John and I had to join him and his son for a meze at the local taverna that afternoon. I had to ring Phyl to ask her not to prepare any dinner for me, again, as we had both got used to these very generous Cypriots. In a way, over that meal, I got to know a lot more about Andros as he just about told us about his life and the horses he owned. I had got the idea I was about to become his farrier for the rest of his racehorses.

Phyl's Art

Before we moved to Cyprus full-time, we had visited the picturesque village of Lania when on holiday. Lania is located on the road from Limassol to the Troodos Mountains and consists of two or three tavernas and several artists who have their paintings on display. Phyl took a liking to one artist called Michael Owen (not the footballer). We even bought two paintings from him and never imagined that we would become good friends with him when we would finally retire to the island.

Michael's paintings were a variety of Cypriot landscape scenes and one that caught my eye was a painting of a Cyprus aircraft in a derelict state that had laid on the runway of the old Nicosia airport since the trouble in 1974. Michael was granted special permission to be allowed to paint in the UN controlled zone (the buffer zone). I never expected a few years later I would be shoeing a horse near to this aircraft. I was more interested in the history of the aircraft but Phyl admired his painting style and the colours and techniques.

Over the years we had visited Michael and his wife Jacky's home several times. On one occasion, he told Phyl he did art lessons now and then and did she want to be put on his list as he didn't advertise and only a select few got asked. A year must have gone by when he sent her an email asking would she like to attend, although I think he had to be persuaded. The first painting she did with Michael was of almond blossom. She felt her painting skills had gone up a notch with the different techniques that Michael taught. I had to agree as we had that almond blossom painting in a frame on our living room wall for a few years and it was admired by many folk. Years later, Phyl put it on display at an exhibition and it won first prize for the category it was entered in.

Over the years, Phyl has sold lots of her pictures but we had hung onto the almond blossom, more for sentimental value. At another exhibition years later, she decided to put it on display and let it go with a big price tag attached to it. We never expected in a million years that, although the painting would be of interest, it would sell at the asking price and to our surprise it did.

Another time, Michael invited us to one of his own exhibitions and we didn't realise that some very rich important people were on the invitation list. I never expected to be chatting with the president of Cyprus with a glass of wine in our hands. I couldn't believe that with Phyl's artwork and my shoeing of horses, we would be at functions were only the gentry of Cyprus would be attending. The evening we attended Michael and Jacky's, we had Phyl's friend, Pam, staying and although I don't think she was an art buff, she couldn't believe who she was socialising with on her holiday.

I got introduced to another artist who told me to call him Eric because that was what his Cypriot name translated to. Eric owned a horse that I used to shoe along with one of his mate's horses. I just thought art was Eric's hobby until his mate told me Eric did it for a living and was an accomplished artist. It was while

I shod Eric's horse, I had mentioned to Eric that Phyl painted too and her paintings that week were on show at an exhibition at the Emplo, a building on Paphos harbour. At the time, Phyl and other artists shared a studio in Kissonerga village near to Coral Bay. Sure enough, he showed up on the Saturday evening. He was a guy who never criticized any art. Everybody's taste was different but if he liked something he would stand and admire it for a while. The others he would just breeze past if they didn't appeal to him.

With Phyls work, he bought several prints of her paintings and another friend, Ken, he took a liking to his too. I think it was Ken who asked about Eric's work and Eric invited us, plus Margret (Ken's wife), up to his home in the village of Alektora the following Sunday. We had a good idea lunch would be at the small taverna in their village. What we didn't expect was that Eric would insist on paying. He made us feel we were his special guests and the day seemed to go far too quickly.

Ken asked if he would show us some of his work and none of us were expecting what we were about to see. He had a waiting list for commissions and we all could see why. His main work was painting icons. I am not a religious person but I could see why his work sold not for hundreds but for thousands. His wife told us that when he first started out as an artist, he held an exhibition where every single painting got sold. I was so pleased for Phyl that two top artists rated her and Eric was at Michael's exhibition too.

Selling our house

After over 11 years in Cyprus, we thought it may be time to move back to the UK. We were a bit worried about what our house would be worth due to the Greek banks collapsing a few years earlier in 2010. Although it didn't actually affect us banking-wise as we only kept a small amount of money in the Cypriot bank for paying standing orders such as electricity and other services. Where it did hurt us was houses and property values collapsed too and the exchange rate was not good either. Our house had dropped 200,000 euros from what it was worth with the banks collapsing and also at the time the pound was strong against the euro. To make matters worse, estate agents charged 5% plus VAT for selling it. They would give a low estimate of what your home was worth just to encourage a sale as nothing was selling at the time. Well, it didn't matter to them if they sold your house that was once worth 3 or 400,000 euros for 100,000. Five percent commission was still a good pay day for them and they could advertise that they could still get sales. When we moved from Chlorakas to Koili in 2006 we no interest in using an estate agent. We sold that house through an advert in the local paper and luckily made a nice profit although nowhere as much as 200,000 to offset the loss of our Koili home.

Our home at Koili, we bought in a derelict and inhabitable state and refurbished to a luxury home complete with a swimming pool and guest apartment. The garden had four lemon trees, a pomegranate tree, a nectarine tree, a fig tree, plus a grapevine. It felt like heaven to me. The views over the valley below were breath taking. We could watch buzzards and sometimes eagles hovering in the sky ready to swoop down on their prey. I thought of the time when I started out in business with no money and could hardly afford the rent for our council house. A place like this in the sun felt a million miles away then. At that time, I wondered if I would be ever able to afford a small cheap terrace house down a narrow street in the UK, never mind a property in a foreign country.

We had had various estate agents round to value our home and we got quite a shock in the wide variety of estimates. From the lowest to the highest there was a €75,000 price difference. Of course, we were more attracted to the estate agent who gave the biggest value but it was well short of what our home was worth a few years before. At the time, it was all ifs and buts if the housing market was ever going to ever pick up. What if it went down and we would never be able to get a sale? Estate agents kept bringing potential clients who would give us the feeling that they were very interested then we wouldn't hear from them ever again. Often, we got the feeling some folk only wanted to come for a nose round until they caught their holiday flight back home.

Then late one afternoon we heard someone shout from outside our garden gate. First we thought was it had nothing to do with us but this shout persisted.

Phyl went to check and sure enough it was a man and his wife shouting for us. I think they thought it best not to come through the gate into the garden as they had seen Jack, our Bearded Collie, wandering about just in case he wasn't friendly.

Yes, this couple had heard on the grapevine our home was on the market. The trouble was they had arrived just at the wrong time for us. We didn't want to put them off and had to apologise because we had just had our dinner. I was in clothes which I had shod a horse in earlier in the day. I didn't know if this couple were horsey or animal lovers, but I apologised in case they got a whiff of the aromas of a burnt horse's hoof embedded in my attire. Not to mention dobs of paint splattered on my hands from just painting a door. The drive was littered with a few lemons that had fallen off the trees and the swimming pool was ready for its weekly clean. The kitchen worktops had dishes, plates and saucepans stacked, ready to be washed, as we had just finished our dinner. Usually, we were given notice from estate agents that they had folk interested in a viewing. That was when we would scramble to have the place looking immaculate with no dirty pots waiting to be washed up. The swimming pool would be looking crystal clear and dropped lemons would have got picked up off the drive. I would not be dressed in smelly work clothes and wouldn't have painted a door five minutes before a viewing.

I think the couple had realised it was perhaps a bad time for us. We were hoping, regardless of the fact they had caught us off-guard, that they could see through the muck and bullets. I tried not to get too close in case I was smelly. Once or twice I had to say, 'Be careful,' due to the wet paint. On leaving they told us they really liked our house, just like many other folk had. We thought, no way can this couple be interested. We were sure they were just saying they liked our property to be polite. After all, our presentation was not at all good. I had just painted a door with the idea to make it more appealing – I thought I had done the opposite when the paint was still wet. Did they think we were trying to gloss over things that needed more attention? It was not the best way to advertise our house!

The very next day the couple got in touch and made an offer which was more or less the asking price, although it was far short of what our property was worth once. The other plus was we hadn't got estate agents fees as it was a private sale as none had been involved. Once a sale is agreed in Cyprus, things move very quickly, unlike in the UK.

I couldn't believe in the following six weeks how quickly things moved. In that time, we had flown back to the UK, bought another home in Bridlington, East Yorkshire, and a week later we were back in Cyprus. We had organised Peter Morten removals to collect our furniture who very kindly stored our furniture until our UK home was ready to move into. We knew we had to find accommodation in the UK as house buying seems to get strung out for months. Luckily, one of my sisters owned a bungalow which was unoccupied at the time. She and her husband very kindly let us live in it for three months until the paper work on our home in Bridlington was completed.

I also needed to sell my van which had transported my farrier kit around the length and breadth of Cyprus. It started to worry me a bit as by the last week before we left Cyprus, I hadn't had any interest for it. I was hoping to get 2000 euros for it but if I got offered any offer, even it was less than half, I would have accepted. Thimius, who I knew from our village, knew we were moving back to the UK, and asked, 'Your motor, Mick, is it for sale?'

'It is, Thimius. Do you want to have a test drive?'

So Thimius went off on a test drive and he must have been gone an hour before he got in touch to ask would I accepted 1500 euros. I quickly accepted as I thought that offer was better than nothing at all and was relieved that I had one less thing to worry about.

The other problem was when the contracts were exchanged for the sale of our Cypriot home, we were going to be homeless for a week. Our good friends, Bob and Margret, very kindly offered to let us to stay with them until our departure date.

We had discussed how we would travel back to the UK many times before we decided to sell after living in Cyprus over 11 years in our lovely Cypriot home. We thought it may be a good idea to drive back due to the fact Jack had a history of escaping from cages as we had found out at Yiannis's vet practice on a few occasions. In fact, we both thought it would be an interesting challenge.

We got in touch with Salamis shipping company which transported mainly lorries as their main cargo but took cars too. They also transported passengers and animals and Jack was no problem. I was told the cabins were a bit rough and ready and not to expect it to be a first-class cruise. The food on board was included in the fare and was very good. The only thing that put Phyl off was we were going to be at sea for four days because the ship was going to Israel first. If it was only for a day she would have put up with it as she was not good at sailing. Years ago, she even got sea sick watching *Titanic*. She had looked at flights to Athens and found a Ryanair flight for 26 euros against 220 for the fare on the ship. We found that her flight got to Athens at 11am on a Sunday morning and the ship docked at 7am, giving me ample time for the three quarter of an hour drive from the docks to the airport. In that time, I would be able to stop somewhere to give Jack a good walk before meeting Phyl.

When our Cypriot home got sold we were going to be homeless for a week! Bob and Margret very kindly offered us to stay with them. The other worry was we realised we had more belongs than we thought and wondered how we would it fit into our two-year-old Suzuki Swift. That was until we thought of vacuum packing our clothes so we could get more stuff into our two suitcases, plus two smaller cabin cases. The largest of the cases was so heavy that it took two of us to lift it into the car. It just fit in behind the back seat. The other one went standing on its end in the foot well of the back seats. The smaller half of the back seat was dropped down with two very full cabin cases in its place. Jack had the larger part of the seat to sit on. Not to mention any spare space was stuffed with tins of dog food and many other things that we couldn't get in the suitcases. Also, two computers were stuffed under the front seats. Not to mention a full rucksack and fleeces piled high in the foot well of Jack's seat. In other words, if there was a gap it got filled with something. Now we hoped nothing went wrong on our 2000-mile journey to the UK.

Some folk had told us we were mad and that in Greece and Italy the car drivers drove like lunatics and asked if we were safe from getting robbed. Well, we didn't get robbed and as for lunatic car drivers, I never saw any difference to the ones in the UK.

The day came for me to say goodbye to Cyprus and to travel to Limassol to catch the ship to Greece via Israel with Jack. Although I didn't mind not having a first-class cabin, I did have one with a sea view. I did get a shock when I was told dogs were not allowed in the cabins in case they caused damage. My first thought was, *my dog had never done any damage at home,* and when I saw my cabin I was sure he wouldn't have made it worse than it was. The threadbare carpets on the floor had seen a lot better days. The bedding, although clean, had got a duvet that was about ready for the rag bag. The bedside cabinet and little table and chair looked a bit worse for wear. I smiled and thought Jack couldn't make it any worse than it was, even if he tried. It had already happened, either by a human or just worn out through age. He was supposed to live in a cage on the draughty ship's deck.

I had tried to reason with the person in charge of the cabins that Jack didn't do cages but it fell on deaf ears. I did put him in the cage and luckily it was near to my cabin. He hadn't been in it ten minutes when I heard him give out what felt like a bloodcurdling scream. I wasted no time to get to him and found he got his mouth wide open and his jaws stuck in the wire mesh sides. I managed with the help of a young crew member who happened to be on night watch to get his jaws free. I got him out of the cage and said, 'It's a blooming good job rules can be broken on this ship.'

'What do you mean?' he replied.

'In big letters painted across the bridge of the ship, it says "no smoking" and nearly all the crew smoke. That means rules can be broken. Either Jack comes into my cabin, or you let me put him in my car,' I replied sternly.

I wasn't supposed to go onto the deck near the cars and lorries, but my car was on the top deck not too far from my cabin. In a way I felt sorry for this young man later. He really understood my predicament and I had given him my feelings about how my dog was treated on the ship and he had helped me to unfree his jaw from the wire mesh cage. He did let me put Jack in the car and he settled down for that night and every night. Once we reached Israel, most of the lorries left the ship and not much got on.

In Israel the customs people got on to question me and fellow passengers for the reason of my visit to Israel. This was in an office on the deck below mine. One of the cooks from the ship's canteen offered to look after Jack while I had to be interrogated. That is how I will describe it. I had, many years before, travelled to Israel for treatment for psoriasis and could remember getting asked some awkward questions then. I thought I was safe when I said I wasn't getting off the ship but was on the way to Greece with my car. 'Why didn't you fly to Greece and collect your car there?' I was asked by a customs officer who had the knack of making me look guilty.

'He is scared of flying and the ship sails in a loop and he has no choice,' replied one of the crew before I said a word, as if he heard it all before. I was relieved when the customs bloke took the word of the crew member and didn't interrogate me anymore, although I don't mind flying. I didn't let on I was traveling with my dog.

I thanked the cook for looking after Jack and said, 'Those customs people ask some blooming awkward questions.'

'I know. That's why I offered to look after your dog. The less they know about him the better,' he muttered. I think he didn't want them to know Jack was on board through other experiences, even when all the proper paperwork was in order.

Once most of the lorries had left the ship and none got on, the top deck must have been the size of two football pitches and I felt Jack enjoyed stretching his legs better than the confined space next to the ship's canteen. At the first morning at breakfast, there was plenty of choice on offer. Sausages, bacon, eggs and even a vegetarian choice. I asked one of the cooks, 'Can I have three sausages and three slices of bacon and two eggs?'

'Have six of each if you want.'

'Thank you. I wanted to give my dog a slice of bacon and a sausage.'

'Well in that case take a few more sausages and bacon then, your dog is a pleasure to have on board,' he replied.

So Jack got fed sausage and bacon at breakfast for four days. I got the feeling this chef was a dog lover as he did give Jack lots of fuss and kindly offered to look after him when the Israeli customs officer wanted to question me.

ARRIVING IN GREECE

The ship docked bang on time at Lavrium port in Greece at 7am on a Sunday morning and Phyl's flight landed at Athens airport later, around 11am. This would fit in perfectly as it gave ample time to clear passport control which took an hour. The airport was only about three quarters of an hour drive away but before meeting Phyl, I wanted Jack to have a proper walk.

On the way to the airport, I saw a lake with a carpark next to it with paths that led into a small, wooded area. I had started to feel a little sorry for Jack as the only walk he had for four days was around the deck of a cargo ship. I didn't even feel comfortable that he had had to spend the nights on his own in my car, but I suppose that was better than being cooped up in a cage on the draughty ship's deck. In the daytime he spent his time next to me where the lorry driver passengers congregated for a coffee outside the ship's canteen.

After giving Jack a nice walk, the next stop was Athens airport, which was a straightforward drive and there was around half an hour to spare before Phyl's flight arrived. The one thing that bothered me though was it was so hot. I didn't want to park in the open carpark for the sake of Jack but under the overhang of the airport balcony where passengers are picked up and dropped off. Although not ideal for Jack's sake, at least it was out of the full sun. My luck was in with parking limited as a car was pulling out as I pulled in smack bang outside the arrivals hall. I kept going in and checking the monitor to check if the Ryanair flight from Cyprus had arrived. I didn't want to leave Jack for too long with the car's back windows open and full of our luggage. I think it only took Phyl 15 minutes once her flight landed to walking out of the airport as she had only hand luggage.

We knew we had got a problem regarding Jack if we flew back. He would not do cages and would fight his way out no matter how secure it was. Yiannis used to call him Houdini after finding out Jack could escape from his cages at the surgery after having a small operation. We had visions, if we flew back, when the aircraft landed and the cargo hold door opened, the baggage handlers being met by Jack, eager to exit the aircraft on his own. Before we explored the idea of driving back, we had to find places to stay at en route for pet friendly hotels. To our surprise, we discovered that there were loads across Europe. In fact, at some Jack got treated better than us in the way of a pack-up of leftover sausages from the breakfasts.

The first hotel we stayed at in Greece resembled the "*Exotic* Marigold *Hotel*" from the film. Although the staff and hospitality were first-class, the building did need attention. Door handles were hanging off, plaster peeling off the walls and so forth, but they were due to be fixed "tomorrow", after we had left. It was a bit like me before I started to write my books as it wasn't today when I would start but always tomorrow, which lasted

35-odd years. I had visions that years later, the same door handles and so forth would still be going to be fixed tomorrow.

We hadn't booked an evening meal as we were not sure what time we would be checking in. Luckily, near to the hotel there was a restaurant with tables outside. No one seemed to mind Jack and the staff were very helpful. When we had finished eating, we were asked if we wanted a coffee. Phyl likes a decaf coffee as a normal one keeps her awake. The waiter was sorry that the restaurant only served Greek coffee. Phyl knew we had a tin of decaf in the car and we asked the waiter if I could find it would he mind using ours, which he was more than happy to do. I have said before if there was a small space in our car something got squashed into it. Luck was in as I could remember exactly which hole I had stuffed the tin of coffee in.

Next morning we had to travel across the rest of Greece to catch another ferry to Italy. This one we were only on for just under a day. It set sail around midnight and was due to arrive at the port of Ancona in Italy at around 8:30pm. Phyl felt she could put up with that. This ship was a bit more of a luxury than the cargo one from Cyprus. It had got nice cabins, restaurants and shops, bars and sun loungers on the deck. Plus, Jack was allowed to stay with us in our cabin. The cabin furniture and was comfortable and the bedding wasn't fitted with duvets ready for the rag bag. The only thing that bothered me was arriving at 8:30pm at Ancona and we had a three-hour drive to Modena at night. I had heard stories of how the Italian driving was not good. Would it be worse in the dark? The answer was that I have seen more bad drivers in the UK. Good old sat-nav soon had us to our destination and although right near to the hotel we were booked in, the road was closed and the sat-nav didn't want to understand that. Luckily, a young couple who were walking past and spoke English soon sorted us out another route.

Next morning we just happened to mention to the hotel receptionist that at the French port, Jack had to have tapeworm treatment by a vet and passport stamped and proof of a rabies jab. In Cyprus we had made sure we had kept his rabies jab up to date and his passport stamped so that wasn't a problem. The tapeworm treatment had to be administered by a vet and passport stamped between one and five days before traveling to the UK. I thought we would have to start looking for a vet a day or so before we arrived at Calais. Also, some folk liked to scare us by saying the French liked to bump charges up to over 100 euros for worming tablets and stamping the passport. Before we left Cyprus, Yiannis had offered to stamp the passport with a date for when we would be leaving France but surely the authorities would notice my car wouldn't be able to travel that fast.

The receptionist said she knew a vet within walking distance from the hotel and very kindly rang them to see if they could help. Sure enough, they were very willing and we just had to go to the vet's surgery at our convenience. After one or two wrong turns from the receptionist's directions we finally found the vets. The vet and the nurse were very helpful and Jack got his medication at a cost of 15 euros.

We thought we should have spent two or three days at Modena. We found it a beautiful place and I would have loved to have explored the Ferrari museum.

The next part of the journey was through the rest of Italy, all the way through Switzerland and just over the border into France for our next stop for the night. Driving through Switzerland, we both had to admire the scenery. Well, that was when we came out of tunnels that cut through the mountain range. I thought how it was possible to blast through solid rock to create a ten-mile tunnel. That was how long one was. At one place that looked like a tourist attraction, we stopped for a loo break and bought a bread salad roll. I thought if we had another one each we would have to take a second mortgage out to pay for it. The view and scenery more than made up for the expensive bread roll though. In Switzerland the wonderful views we got driving through the mountains (when not in the tunnels) made our journey more enjoyable. We began to wish we had booked two or three days at each hotel instead of one night. I knew we had Jack but with what we know now, all these pet-friendly hotels really loved dogs. If anything, they got more attention than we did. In fact, I think some of the staff preferred dogs to people.

We left the hotel in Italy in the late morning and had arrived in France, just over the border from Switzerland, at around six in the evening where we were booked for the night. The next place, a chateau, was an old, well-maintained building filled with lots of antique furniture. On first impression was we thought we had got the wrong place with Ferraris and other expensive cars in the carpark. The lady who owned the place was very helpful and showed us to our room. Our room consisted of three rooms. A bedroom with a four-poster bed and again with antique furniture. The large bathroom had a chandelier that would have graced a stately home banqueting hall.

Then another door into our private living room, complete with a three-piece-suite and television. We couldn't believe this was priced at less than a Premier Inn. At our evening meal, Jack was laid on a highly polished wooden floor next to our table. When the lady saw him, she decided that Jack may be more comfortable on a rug. She went off and came back with Persian rug for him to lay on. The next morning, Jack had got used to having first-class comfort and we woke up to find him fast asleep in an antique armchair instead of his own bed.

Before breakfast was served, the lady proprietor said we were welcome to give Jack a walk in the chateau estate. The grounds and gardens were nearly the size of a stately home. Again, we wished we hadn't booked in for just the night as the food was first-class and the wine was some of the best I had ever tasted.

The next part of the journey was a 400-plus-mile-drive to a guest house before catching the Eurotunnel train from Calais back to the UK. This drive was on a motorway with not much traffic. At times I had to watch the speed limit as it was very easy for our sporty Suzuki Swift to want to hit the ton. I thought it was the car having a mind of its own as I was sure it had got nothing to do with me. We only stopped twice for refreshment breaks and to fuel the car and let jack stretch his legs. With no traffic to talk of, we made our last stop at a guest house around 4pm. The two guys who ran the place were chefs who had cooked a five-course evening meal for their guests. All I will say about these chaps was they looked as if they liked their food. Judging by the large potions we got served for dinner, I think if we stayed a week our waistline may have expanded a couple of inches. When we got up the next morning, I was not sure if I needed breakfast as I felt the meal the night before had something to do with it. I felt I had eaten enough food to last me for a week. Even going for a walk with Jack I felt I was walking with a waddle from an overly full stomach. Nevertheless, we were treated first-class and Jack was too as all dogs got given a large bag of dog biscuits.

The Eurotunnel at Calais was only a short drive away and we had booked an afternoon train just in case we had problems with Jack. Before we set off, some folk had told us of the red tape we could come up against at Calais. By 10am that morning we had cleared the customs people and it only took a few minutes for Jack's passport and microchip to be checked. I think some of the bad reports we had heard about were from folk who hadn't followed the rules.

Now we were around four hours early but we found for 20 euros we could get on the next shuttle that left in half an hour, although we were nearly the last car to be loaded on the shuttle. An hour later we were driving down the M20 towards London, then on to Phyl's mum in Derbyshire. We had hit the UK after a week and a day of travel without any major problems. We planned to stay with Phyl's mum for one night before travelling up to near Blackpool and meeting up with my sister and husband. They had very kindly let us use their unoccupied bungalow until the sale of our house was finalised.

Our home in Bridlington, East Yorkshire

We had arrived in the UK on the last day of May and only expected to be living in my sister and brother-in-law's bungalow for a month, but it was the end of August when we finally got the keys for our new home. It was in a small, friendly cul-de-sac on the outskirts of Bridlington where all the neighbours knew each other. My sister's bungalow was furnished so we didn't need our own furniture there. Peter Morton's Removals in Cyprus had had kept our furniture in storage for us. They informed us our belonging were on the way to the UK to a firm called Chudley Removals who would deliver it. I think our furniture arrived at Chudley's a day or so before we moved to our new home but they couldn't deliver it until a week later. That meant we were sleeping on a blow-up bed and sitting on two small garden chairs we had bought in Tesco.

Once we were settled in and Chudley's had delivered our furniture, I thought this is definitely retirement. For me, no more horses to shoe, and Phyl had no more accounts to sort out. Both of us could give more time to our hobbies. We both joined Bridlington U3A as there were many art groups Phyl was interested in. With me,

I had got into writing and I thought the U3A may have a writers' group. We found out that once a month they had a general meeting at the Bridlington Spa where guest speakers spoke either about their life or it could be of the life of animals, birds, travel, history and many other topics. Most were interesting but I must confess one or two I found to be very boring, and I was not alone. There were tables with a sheet of paper for folk to enrol at any group attracting new members. You name the group, it was more than likely to be there and if it wasn't, it could be started. In my case, there were no sheets out to join a writers' group. I asked the committee member leader in charge of all the teams, and I asked: 'I was looking for a writers' group. Don't you have one?'

'We have now,' he replied. 'Can you run it?'

So the next meeting I had a sheet of paper on the table, looking for folk interested in forming a writers' group. I did get plenty of interest and Bridlington U3A writers' group was formed. I often thought that a few years earlier, I was the novice writer and now I was in charge. Although it wasn't at the high standard of Paphos as most of the members were not interested if their grammar or dialog quotations, commas, etcetera were important. Lots were like me when I first started to write as I never knew how to operate a computer. Saying that, although their work may not have had commas, chapters, and so forth, their stories were very good and interesting.

Another group we joined was science and technology. It was a new group and the leader wanted everybody in attendance to introduce themselves and say what we had done for a living. Where I was sitting, I was first to be asked and introduced myself with, 'My name is Mick O'Reardon and I was a farrier for 52 years.'

'Really, would you give us a talk?' came the reply from the leader and others. 'That sounds to be interesting and a bit different.'

Phyl was next and said, 'I was an accountant.'

'Oh good. Would you do the U3A books? We haven't got a treasurer.'

We found out later the last treasurer had had a fall out with a committee member and left.

I did give the science and technology members a talk about the ins and outs of horseshoeing and I was surprised to have a full room with standing room only. I had put together on my computer examples and techniques to be transferred to a screen to help explain some of the finer points of farriery. The talk must have lasted two hours and I got good feedback from the many questions I got asked. Many didn't know that so much could be involved in horseshoeing.

Not long after, I got asked if I would give Flamborough Women's Institute a talk too but not the technical side of a farrier. More about my life as a farrier. They didn't want a lecture like I did for the U3A, but more of the amusing and not so amusing things that had happened when shoeing horses. I had got the feeling my farrier life was not quite over yet.

Phyl did become the U3A treasurer. When she took on the role there was around 700 members and it took only an hour or so a week and she had to attend committee meetings once a month. Two years later, more folk had joined, with a membership of around 1400, so more work for her. What started as an hour or so a week, now turned into an hour a day.

FARRIER PROBLEMS

After Phyl and I had returned to the UK, I learnt there were problems farrier-wise in Cyprus. Pat had started asking me what could be wrong with Mac's hooves and several other horse owners had sent photos asking me for advice. After several phone calls from Pat and now Wendy, they were thinking of flying me back out to Cyprus, and I thought I had fully retired. I even took the photos I had got sent for a second opinion off Doug Bradbury, a top UK farrier and a friend I had known for 30-plus years. In Cyprus the hooves get rock-hard and any excess sole is very hard to trim off. I wanted a second opinion as sometimes a photo of a horse's hoof may not be as bad when seen on the actual horse. My diagnoses was there was excess sole to be trimmed off. When this was done, the farrier would see that the hoof wall would have more growth that was not visible. So, with not getting rid of the dead sole, the shoes would get fitted over the overgrown hoof. Doug agreed with me, although it can be difficult to diagnose when you are 2000 miles away from the horse.

I had a trick, and I am sure one or two other farriers know of it, if the rock-hard sole is difficult to pare off. That is to have a blow lamp and blow the hot flame over the sole of the hoof. I don't mean to keep it aimed at one place on the horse's foot but to waft the flame about. Once that is done for around 30 seconds to a minute, the sole becomes soft enough to trim with ease. Sometimes try a hot shoe as if you are fitting it as that often works too. From what I had seen, and Doug agreed with me, all that needed to be done was to get rid of any excessive sole and be able to trim the wall of the hoof to its natural level. A horse's hoof is more than likely to crack and break up, especially in very dry atmosphere, just like a human's long fingernail if left too long.

In 2018, I was all set to fly to Cyprus as Pat and many others had started to ask for my advice. Then a new farrier appeared on the island. Pat told me when he shod her horses, there were lots of hoof clippings on the ground, unlike the farrier before. I was relieved that my idea was correct, and I didn't hear of any more complaints until we went on holiday to Cyprus in 2019.

Horseshoeing and the hustle and bustle of stable life is still a big interest to me. It is the physical bit my body was telling me to stop doing. I found I was not as strong as I used to be. Well, on that holiday where did I find myself, yes, up at Pat's Aphrodite Hills riding school! On that occasion, Emily and Helen were there as they helped out at Pat's too. I had hardly got out of the car when I had Emily more or less dragging me out of the car door to inspect Troy's hind feet. She wanted to know the reason why his hinds were turning out as he had always walked straight. Once I had inspected, I noticed both the outside branch wall was shod a lot higher than the inner branch wall. It would be like a human walking with stone in their shoes on the outside of their foot. All the weight was forced onto the inside of the foot and they would have had no choice to walk splay-footed.

Pat told me she had the farrier booked a couple of days later and would I like to meet him. He only had a pair of fronts to fit on one of her young horses. Emily had said he could be mighty slow as it took him around two-plus hours to shoe Troy but I thought it may have felt two hours to her.

Two days later, I arrived at Pat's before the farrier. When he arrived, they had already told him I wanted to meet him. The first thing he did was to show me the kit he had in his van. You name the tools, he had them. I am not sure if lots of them had ever got used. Then he got out is phone me to show me photos of horses that he had shod. Finally, he started to put front shoes on Pat's youngster that looked to be getting fed up waiting. When Emily had earlier told me he took an age to shoe her horse, I didn't expect him to be at Pat's for over two hours just to fit a pair of fronts. He showed me all the fancy gear he got in his van and could talk forever on different horseshoeing problems. When I inspected this young horse's front feet after he had dressed them ready for fitting the shoe, I pointed out they were not dressed level. One heel was a lot higher than the other, just like on Troy. He said to me, 'Mick, I am was sure it will be OK when fitted.'

'I can assure you it's not OK when fitted. Later on in this young horse's life it may cause problems if not fitted level,' I said, alarmed.

'It will wear level naturally, trust me,' he said, trying his hardest to justify that the foot being level was not important.

With that he went and got a T square from his van which looked as if he had never used it until now and wanted to prove me wrong. He lifted the horse's leg and seemed confident that he was right. I was praying he was wrong. 'How can you see that, Mick? You are right,' he asked with a surprised look on his face. What surprised me was he never put the problem right and just nailed the shoes on!

I didn't need a T square to check if the foot was level. All that is needed is to have a good eye and this time anybody would have noticed the heels were far from level. It wasn't as if this horse wanted remedial shoeing and I could now see what had happened with Troy and several others when I was asked for an opinion.

I must say, I think it showed I was not impressed with this guy and a couple of years later I got more photos and X-rays of a horse's feet and this time it was Troy. A vet I had briefly met just before I left Cyprus, who was more up to date with modern equine procedures, was making a good name for himself. Emily had got in touch with this vet as Troy was not sound. He thought all that was wrong was Troy's hooves were not balanced. He had taken an X-ray, more just to eliminate any other concerns but was sure it was more likely to be how Troy was shod. I had to agree with the vet after studying the photos and X-rays Emily had sent me in a messenger post. Again, the heels didn't look anywhere near level and X-rays didn't show anything major that could be causing problems. Emily then started sending me photos of who her friends used as a farrier and asked me which farrier I thought would shoe Troy the best.

Now Troy is shod better and he hasn't suffered any sign of lameness. Mind you, I did get a long, drawn-out message from the guy explaining his reason why Troy needed to be shod like he was. He was trying to blame the hard ground, not his work. Now I often think if only I was 30 years younger I could have earned a fortune in Cyprus.

I still like to attend any horseshoeing competitions as a spectator and have a natter with other farriers. I think Phyl may be right when she says that when farriers get together at dinners or any other functions we get more horses shod in one evening than in a week's work by just talking horseshoeing.

Yes, I am sure I have fully retired from working as a farrier. I have enjoyed all my working life and felt lucky to have met other very highly trained farriers who became my friends. I think it is definitely time to hang up my hammer and enjoy retirement. Who knows what the future holds – will I get withdrawal symptoms and do a bit more farrier work? I don't think I will. But...

Milton Keynes UK
Ingram Content Group UK Ltd.
UKHW032049201124
451474UK00005B/337